TRAGEDY IN
THE VICTORIAN NOVEL

To my Mother and Father

TRAGEDY
IN THE
VICTORIAN NOVEL

THEORY AND PRACTICE IN
THE NOVELS OF
GEORGE ELIOT, THOMAS HARDY
AND HENRY JAMES

JEANNETTE KING

CAMBRIDGE UNIVERSITY PRESS

CAMBRIDGE
LONDON   NEW YORK   MELBOURNE

Published by the Syndics of the Cambridge University Press
The Pitt Building, Trumpington Street, Cambridge CB2 1RP
Bentley House, 200 Euston Road, London NW1 2DB
32 East 57th Street, New York, NY 10022, USA
296 Beaconsfield Parade, Middle Park, Melbourne 3206, Australia

First published 1978
First paperback edition 1979

First printed in Great Britain by
Western Printing Services Ltd, Bristol
Reprinted in Great Britain by Redwood Burn Ltd, Trowbridge & Esher

Library of Congress Cataloguing in Publication Data

King, Jeanette.

Tragedy in the Victorian novel.

Based on the author's thesis, Aberdeen.

Bibliography: p.

Includes index

1. English fiction – 19th century – History and
criticism. 2. Tragic, The. 3. Eliot, George, pseud.,
i.e. Marian Evans, afterwards Cross, 1819–80 –
Criticism and interpretation. 4. Hardy, Thomas
1840–1928 – Criticism and interpretation. 5. James, Henry,
1843–1916 – Criticism and interpretation. I. Title.
PR878.T7K5   823.'03   77–77762

ISBN 0 521 21670 2 hard covers
ISBN 0 521 29744 3 paperback

CONTENTS

v

PREFACE

Critics today, without any apparent sense of incongruity, frequently refer to 'tragic novels'. They do not have the critical inhibitions of their Victorian counterparts, who were more aware of the possible conflict between the ancient concept of tragedy and the relatively new genre of the novel. What, then, do we mean when we yoke together the two terms? Tragedy is now a word used by everyone to refer to many kinds of unfortunate incident. But does it still possess any of the formal implications of the drama from which the term originated?

I have chosen to concentrate my discussion of the relationship between tragedy and the Victorian novel on George Eliot, Thomas Hardy and Henry James, because they were consistently preoccupied with the idea of tragedy, both in life and in art. George Eliot's interest in tragic themes, particularly in relation to pathos, is apparent in almost all her novels. In Hardy's case, it is the four later novels which are most clearly experiments with both the idea and the form of tragedy. James's early, shorter works show a tension between 'modern' and traditional concepts of tragedy which is carried forward into the later, major fiction. But in *The Wings of the Dove* and *The Portrait of a Lady* James extends his preoccupation with tragedy until it encompasses form as well as theme.

Hardy, James and Eliot are major novelists, but not the least of their achievements is the light they shed on the whole concept of tragedy. In this respect, their works involve us in a process of redefinition and critical enquiry.

A number of critics have written on the tragic elements in the work of these novelists. Among the most illuminating are Barbara Hardy on George Eliot, John Paterson on Hardy, and Frederick Crews on Henry James. I am indebted to these and to the many more listed in the Bibliography who touch on related issues.

I owe a more direct debt to Professor Andrew Rutherford of the University of Aberdeen for his invaluable advice during the writing of the thesis from which this book emerged. Finally I would like to express my gratitude to the late T.R. Henn, whose teaching and friendship provided so much encouragement when the ideas for this book were still taking shape.

INTRODUCTION
THE CRITICAL BACKGROUND

George Eliot's novels are not novels in the ordinary sense of the term – they are really dramas: as the word is understood when applied to *Hamlet* or *The Agamemnon*.

    (Anon. review of '*Felix Holt*', *Westminster Review*, 86, 1866, p. 200.)

In this novel [*The Mill on the Floss*] therefore, we have reproduced the grand old element of interest which the Greek drama possessed, the effect of circumstances upon man; but you have, in addition, that analysis of the inner mind, of which *Hamlet* stands in literature the greatest example.

    (Anon. review of '*The Mill on the Floss*', *Spectator*, 7 Apr. 1860, p. 331.)

Mr Thomas Hardy's new novel is as pitiless and tragic in its intensity as the old Greek dramas.   (H.W. Massingham, 'Mr. Hardy's New Novel'
Daily Chronicle, 28 Dec. 1891, p. 3.)

Tess must take its place among the great tragedies.

    (W. Watson, '*Tess of the D'Urbervilles*,' *Academy*, 41, 1892, p. 125.)

Jude the Obscure gives the sense of the return of an English writer to the Greek motive of tragedy.   (W.D. Howells, '*Jude the Obscure*', *Harper's Weekly*, 7 Dec. 1895, p. 1156.)

Henry James suddenly brings us, for all his gentleness and urbanity, upon tragedy of the highest order.   (S. Waterlow, 'The Work of Mr. Henry James', *Independent Review*, 4. 1904, p. 243.)

Such comparisons of the novel with tragedy became so common by the middle of the nineteenth century as to suggest an important literary trend. Samuel Richardson had already likened the novel to tragedy as early as 1748 in his 'Postscript' to *Clarissa*, but it was only the later discussions which related to central conceptions of the status and function of the novelist's art. These discussions show, in particular, a growing awareness that a literary transition was taking place, that one dominant mode – tragedy – was giving

way to another – the novel. And the later genre was attempting
to do, in a new and often controversial way, many of the things
that the older genre had done.

But what did the word 'tragedy' mean to those who used it in
relation to the novel? It was frequently used, as it is today, to
mean an extremely sad and unexpected event. In fiction, as in
life, it usually meant death or some equally final disaster. For
many writers, however, this single event illustrated the nature of
life in general, a pattern of continuous and inevitable – *not* unexpected – suffering. For them 'tragedy' suggested a vision of
life, a tragic philosophy, and it is in just such philosophical and
moral terms that the comparison between tragedy and the novel is
most often made.

To writers like George Eliot and Anthony Trollope, the
traditionally ennobling effect of tragedy on humanity represented
an ideal of the affective power of literature; it also represented,
therefore, a model for the moral status and function of the novel.
They believed that tragic drama had, in fact, been supplanted by
the novel as the mirror of life and as a teaching form. This attitude could obviously lead to an over-concentration on the didactic
qualities of a novel. One anonymous reviewer's sole criterion for
praising a novel called *The Trials of Margaret Lyndsay*, by a
certain John Wilson, was that it illustrated 'situations of sorrow
and affliction, calculated to strengthen, by their example, the
patience, the resignation, and the pity of the unfortunate'.[1] A
more imaginative and rewarding approach to the novel's 'lessons'
was taken by the critic George Brimley, who stressed the wide
range of experience the novel offers us, making us 'live in the
lives of other types of character than our own, or than those of
our daily acquaintance – to enable us to pass by sympathy into
other minds and other circumstances, and especially to train the
moral nature by sympathy with noble characters and noble
actions'.[2] The term 'noble' reminds us of the classical tragic
models, and was to prove a controversial point, but the link
between literature as vicarious experience and moral education

had a more immediate ancestry in the Romantic tradition. It is the basis of Shelley's argument that the imagination is a great moral instrument. George Eliot's aim of extending our sympathies is an echo of William Wordsworth's desire to convey the experience of common people in *The Lyrical Ballads*. So important was the concept of moral education to considerations of the novel's function that 'seriousness' became a key-word for literary judgment, as for many critics it still is.

But the battle against those who believed that the novel's job was to entertain, not teach, was not over. As late as 1890, most people saw the novel as primarily a source of amusement, as many still do. Romance became increasingly popular. The growing divide between critical and popular taste is illustrated in the critic W.E. Henley's scathing comment on the public reception of George Meredith's *Rhoda Fleming* (1889): 'the emotions developed are too tragic, the personages too elementary in kind and too powerful in degree, the effects too poignant and too sorrowful' for a public whom it irks 'to grapple with problems capable of none save a tragic solution'.[3]

Even those who agreed that the novel should teach disagreed over what it should teach. Many felt that while it should certainly 'grapple with problems', it ought to come up with something better than a 'tragic solution'. Pessimism was particularly abhorrent to such critics, which made Thomas Hardy's novels a frequent target for abuse. They insisted that tragedy – however 'true' – had no place in the novel, and seemed to question the validity of tragedy itself as a literary form. But the problem here is again one of definition. The frequent demands that the novel should satisfy the instinct for poetic justice remind us again of the neo-classical models and theories which formed the attitudes to tragedy of so many nineteenth-century critics, and so often had a limiting effect on early criticism of the novel.

For, to most critics, tragedy still meant Greek tragedy. And Greek tragedy more often seemed to mean the *Poetics* of Aristotle than the actual drama of Aeschylus, Sophocles or Euripides.

Dramatic criticism in England had, from its birth, been classical and Aristotelian, and remained so throughout the sixteenth and seventeenth centuries, in spite of the successful and radically different practice of Shakespearean tragedy, more influenced by Seneca and the Romans than by the Greeks. Sir Philip Sidney, Ben Jonson and Milton each rejected the 'low' and comic elements of contemporary drama. With the Baroque tragedy of the seventeenth century, classicism really came into its own. Dramatists like Milton and Dryden, and Corneille and Racine in France, imposed limitations on themselves which were more rigid than the 'conventions' outlined by Aristotle, so that the tension between passion and the severe control of high art became their distinguishing characteristic. The logical conclusion of this increasingly scholastic, decreasingly lively tradition was the 'closet' drama of the nineteenth century. The neo-classical drama of Swinburne, Arnold and Tennyson in particular can hardly have been intended for performance, and needed long prefaces to explain the increasingly obscure classical sources.

But in spite of the evidence that new forms of tragedy were required, critics still clung to such supposedly Aristotelian concepts as the noble, majestic hero, poetic justice, the cathartic ending and the rejection of 'low' characters. Aristotle certainly suggested that the characters in tragedy should be 'good', that is the finest of their type or class, and that the hero in particular should be 'highly renowned and prosperous'.[4] The novelist, therefore, who chooses to make his hero a common man is faced with the problem of finding compensating factors for the loss of the (symbolic) values that derive from the hero's identification with the fate of his people. But the hero was not to be wholly good, or his ruin would be simply repugnant and horrible rather than tragic. He had to make the infamous tragic error or *hamartia*. Aristotle seems to have meant by this simply a mistake, making the hero's fate logical and convincing, but not necessarily just. His interest in *peripeteia* (reversal) and *anagnorisis* (recognition) shows that his main concern is not with drama that illustrates poetic justice in its simplest form, the punishment of evil-doing. A *peripeteia* occurs when a course of action intended to produce result x produces the reverse of x. The deepest tragedy occurs when a man's destruction is the work of those that wish him well, or of his own unwitting hand. But *hamartia* was so often misinterpreted as 'moral flaw' that there was a consequent emphasis on the notion of poetic justice. For disaster to overtake the morally innocent was to the neo-classicists not tragic, but pathetic. Tragedy should excite pity and fear. A common criticism of the nineteenth-century novel was that it excited too much pity, destroying the tension necessary to tragedy.

Although using slightly different terms, George Saintsbury is clearly making the same distinction when he distinguishes tragic pathos from sentimental pathos by an 'adequate, necessary and just'[5] connection between cause and effect. Without this relationship, the irony essential to tragedy cannot exist. What Saintsbury failed to see was that, for a writer like Hardy, irony exists in the protagonist's mistaken belief in a relationship between cause and effect which he can control. And even if causal guilt is absent, he may bear a degree of impersonal responsibility, of moral and aesthetic appropriateness, which is in itself tragic.

Was there no mitigating influence in favour of realism and contemporary subjects from the successful body of Shakespearean drama with which every Englishman was familiar? This native version of tragedy strongly reinforced the concept of poetic justice which later critics read into the Aristotelian tragic theory. The evil in the Shakespearean world-picture is very clearly generated by sin, rather than a simple mistake. But this emphasis on sin also places an emphasis on the tragedy of character which is missing from the classical 'tragedies of situation'.

This kind of interest in the individual's responsibility for his own tragedy is shown in the exploration which so many nineteenth-century novelists, particularly those at the centre of this study, made of the relationship between determinism and free will. What is it that makes some people complete victims of their situation, and others able to endure, and even triumph over it? Similarly, the heroic, as well as the tragic, element is related to character rather than situation. Shakespearean tragedy concerns characters to whom it is proper to do honour, but the honour can belong to the hero not only by birthright, but by achievement.

Such stature was necessary to make the lesson of tragedy plain, to give the hero's actions a wider significance. But it was also related to the function of the 'low' or comic elements which most clearly differentiate this body of tragedy from the classical model. It is the contrasts between, and mirroring of, the 'high' and 'low' elements that give Shakespearean tragedy its depth and universality. But this argument for introducing low elements into tragedy, in spite of the brilliantly successful examples it provided, is ignored by those critics who attack similar elements in tragic novels. They frequently compare the nineteenth-century novel with Shakespearean drama. George Eliot's portrayal of rustic characters and of realistic, homely, humorous dialogue, is described, like Hardy's, with delight and admiration. But in tragedy, such elements are still suspect. It has to be admitted that humble characters are present in Shakespearean tragedy as contrast, not as potentially heroic or tragic elements. But it seems an indication of the critics' extremely static, backward-looking approach that so many were unable to see the Victorian novelists as merely taking the native, rather than classical, tradition one step further. On the whole, most of them seem to take one step back, neglecting Shakespeare's tragedy as a model for tragedy, while accepting his work as a fruitful model for comedy.

With its emphasis on the nobly heroic, undertaking great actions of high moral seriousness, the tragic ideal was, then, for many critics, totally incompatible with realism, which was concerned with what Engels called 'typical characters in typical situations'.[6] The attempt of George Eliot to pivot tragedy on the experience of humble characters seemed futile to a critic like J. Herbert Stack.

Despite all the efforts of the greatest novelist of our days, the tragedy of Hetty Poyser's [sic] life does not touch us nearly as the same sorrow in one of higher station. It is simply cant for educated men to pretend that their sentiments are as easily excited by the sorrows of people whose daily life and daily thoughts they can with difficulty realise, as by the sufferings of those who, on account of their nearness to us in social position, seem like ourselves, and whose sorrows we can understand and feel.

('Mr. Anthony Trollope's Novels', *Fortnightly Review*, 5, 1869, p. 191.)

Wordsworth's attempts to educate his public in this direction had apparently failed. Few would disagree with the belief that sympathy is essential to tragedy, but can the novelist extend the reader's sympathy across social and class barriers? Aesthetic theory becomes involved with moral and social attitudes at this point. Many realistic novelists felt themselves to be attacking not merely literary conventions but the moral sense of their readers.

But the arguments of those who hold Stack's position cannot be dismissed purely as a kind of literary snobbery. Such a position clearly relates to those qualities of the tragic hero and the tragic action outlined above. The fate of the private, and in particular the working-class, individual lacks the significance attaching to that of the 'highly renowned', majestic and exceptional hero of Aristotle's *Poetics*. And critics were quick to recognise that the absence of these traditional majestic qualities was due to the underlying philosophy of the realists. R.H. Hutton, one of the most important and perceptive of Victorian critics, blamed Hardy's fatalism.

Tragedy is almost impossible to people who feel and act as if they were puppets of a sort of fate. Tragedy gives us the measure of human greatness, and elevates us by giving it in the very moment when we sound the depth of human suffering. Mr Hardy's tragedy seems carefully limited to gloom. It gives us the measure of human miserableness, rather than of human grief – of the incapacity of man to be great in suffering, or anything else.

('*The Return of the Native*', *Spectator*, 8 Feb. 1879, p. 182.)

These, then, are the many reasons put forward for considering the lower classes inappropriate subjects for tragedy. Their social

position deprives their fall of any wider significance, and therefore of any element of real catastrophe. And their limited mental
range deprives their suffering of any greatness.

It is undeniable that the portrayal of tragedy through humble
characters raises many difficulties – some perhaps insoluble – but
they are of a more practical kind than those raised by critics
seeking a direct equivalent of the classical form. Even George
Henry Lewes, one of the great champions of realism and the man
who persuaded George Eliot to try writing fiction, points out that
'it is easy for the artist to choose a subject from everyday life, but
it is *not* easy for him so to represent the characters and their
actions that they shall be at once lifelike and interesting'.[7] In
such mundane, limited spheres, truth can be dangerously close to
boredom. The problem reveals itself most acutely in the representation of dialogue. It is forcibly expressed by Biffen, the realist
novelist in George Gissing's *New Grub Street* (1893). He wishes
to reproduce verbatim the conversation of working people: 'The
result will be something unutterably tedious. Precisely. That is
the stamp of the ignobly decent life. If it were anything *but*
tedious it would be untrue' (p. 129). How is the novelist to remain faithful to this quality of tedium, which disastrously weakens
the impact of his art, yet is the essence of the tragedy he wishes to
portray?

Moreover, the language of such characters lacks that eloquent
special pleading characteristic of the traditional tragic hero. How,
then, is their suffering, their passion, to be conveyed? Even for
novelists writing about upper-class characters, realism created
similar problems. It is not so much that their characters cannot
express themselves as that – in the rarefied atmosphere of civilised
society – they dare not. The 'tea-pot style of conversation'[8] in
Henry James's novels seemed to many critics to make his characters unreal, lacking in flesh and blood. W.E. Henley felt that
this 'new American method' might be effective in the representation of the commonplace, but was hopelessly inadequate when
applied to the tragic.

In Mrs. Malet's heroine there is a touch of something very much like tragedy; and we feel as we read that she ought to have been presented to us ten years ago...We are confronted with reticences and delicacies, with shyness and discretion and significant silence, when we are crying out for courage and free speech and the note of passion and all the majesty of truth. ('New Novels', *Academy*, 22, 1882, p. 377.)

But whether the novelist chose to write about working-class or upper-class characters, he was liable to criticism if he attempted to relate tragedy to everyday experience. In his strictures on *The Return of the Native* already quoted, R.H. Hutton went on to criticise it for treating 'tragedy itself as hardly more than a deeper tinge of the common leaden-colour of the human lot, and so makes it seem less than tragedy – dreariness, rather than tragedy' p. 181. 'Dreariness' is a word similarly applied by many to James's novels. Such views are clearly at odds with those of novelists like George Eliot, who see the elements of tragedy everywhere, who see tragedy as a universal experience. The classicist's demand was for the exceptional, the heroic gesture, the hero in active conflict with the universe. Matthew Arnold's description of those situations which can give no poetical enjoyment could aptly be applied to many Victorian tragic novels – 'those in which the suffering finds no vent in action; in which a continuous state of mental distress is prolonged, unrelieved by incident, hope, or resistance; in which there is everything to be endured, nothing to be done'.[9] But could it not equally be applied to the last act of *King Lear*?

No issue illustrated the gulf between the traditionalists and modernists more than that of the ending. I have already mentioned the neo-classicist's desire for poetic justice. Those who, in addition, sought that cathartic experience of 'calm of mind, all passion spent', which accompanies the resolution of classical tragic drama, were repeatedly frustrated in their readings of contemporary novels. The frequent absence of finality robbed them not only of the moral satisfaction of seeing poetic justice meted out and the restoration of stability, but of the aesthetic pleasure of wholeness. Henry James was, again, frequently singled out for his refusal to provide any resolution, tragic or otherwise. R.H. Hutton expressed the feelings of many.

Mr. Henry James is always more or less embarrassed by what he very likely regards as the artificial necessity of making a whole. He finds that life very seldom makes a whole. If you may trust him as your guide, even human passion is not commonly dramatic. It ends oftener in a ravelled thread than in a true dénouement. . .In his pictures most passions fade away; most tragedies break down before the tragic crisis.

(Review of '*Washington Square*', *Spectator*, 5 Feb. 1881, p. 185.)

Although prepared to acknowledge James's power of suggesting the continuity of things, such critics were not prepared to acknowledge the place of continuity in tragedy. The audience may be aware of life continuing at the end of tragedy, but it is life purged of the suffering that in James belongs to the continuing existence, so that the audience is more conscious of climax than continuity.

If attempts to create tragedy out of such 'realistic' subject-matter were not always acceptable, then neither were the realist methods adopted to portray them. Many critics felt the particularity with which character was rendered in so many Victorian novels was incompatible with the representative function of the tragic hero. It obscured the vast, elemental forces within and without him. Similar reservations were expressed about the often highly detailed background of the novels. G.H. Lewes warned that realism should not become 'detailism': if the novelist wants to portray a human tragedy, 'the upholsterer must be subordinate, and velvet must not draw our eyes away from faces'.[10]

All too often such criticisms reveal a total misunderstanding of the author's purpose. James is criticised for his too frequent tendency to 'immerse his drama in a saturated atmosphere of convention',[11] by an anonymous reviewer who has failed to understand the nature of these drawing-room tragedies. James – like Racine – uses social convention as a barrier between the individual and the release of his feelings, increasing by such pressure the

that's good

intensity of restrained grief. Similarly, R.H. Hutton writes of /
Middlemarch:

it could hardly be a satisfying imaginative whole, either tragic or otherwise; for the object is to paint not the grand defeat, but the helpless en-
tanglement and miscarriage of noble aims; to make us see the eager
stream of high purpose, not leaping destructively from the rock, but more
or less silted up, though not quite lost, in the dreary sands of modern life.

('*Middlemarch*', *British Quarterly Review*, 57, 1873, p. 408.)

He failed to see in Dorothea's experience what a more acute critic
saw in Rosamund's, that it was 'even more intensely tragical in
being veiled throughout in garments of common life and never
revealed to the common eye'.[12] Few critics seemed able, however,
to penetrate the veil or to see how essential it was to the author's
vision of modern tragedy. Few saw how vital not only to her
method but to her meaning it was that all extremes of suffering
or greatness should be almost hidden in the welter of everyday
realities.

The differences in method and form between the novel and
tragic drama were, therefore, frequently used as the clinching
argument for the unsuitability of the novel as a tragic medium. At
its crudest, this was based on the simple assertion that the more
obvious formal structure of drama was innately superior to that
of the novel. But G.H. Lewes countered that the novel could and
should share the structural ideal of drama – economy and a story
free from anything superfluous. The production of so many in-
ferior novels could, he felt, be blamed partly on just those critics
who set lower standards for the novel than for the drama, failing
to take the younger form seriously as art. The most constructive
criticism comes from those who distinguished between those
novels that were significantly 'dramatic', and could fruitfully be
compared structurally with tragic drama, and those that were not.
But it is rare for any critic to ask the most important question in
connection with the novel's form. Do the formal and structural
aspects of drama, referred to by the classicists with such praise,
express in a unique way the themes and philosophy of tragedy?

Only the answer to this will tell us whether or not drama is the essential medium for the tragic vision, an integral element of tragedy.

One of the most illuminating and comprehensive comments to come from those critics demanding the stylised, formal and structural qualities of traditional tragedy came from Henry H. Lancaster. Lancaster was ostensibly attacking George Eliot's novels on the grounds of the inadequacy of her lower-class characters, but his comments on Greek tragedy tell us much more about the grounds for his objections. Concerned as it was with 'the actions of the gods, at best of demi-gods and heroes', Greek tragedy was – in comparison with modern tragedy – '*alien* from humanity, and appeals to our sense of the terrible and the sublime'.[18] To such critics, tragedy was a highly distanced form of art, rejecting the everyday, the contemporary and the immediate. That is, it was a form completely dissociated from any tragic experience in real life. As a *Guardian* critic put it, most revealingly:

> manifest power and much accompanying beauty will not reconcile most of us to the continued strain on our feelings, when tragedy is represented, not among heroes whose loftiness seems to make them fit for it, but among ordinary people of our own mould and time. It is *too near the truth* which we are familiar with to be agreeable even in fiction.
> (Anon. review of '*The Mill on Floss*', The Guardian, 25 Apr. 1860, p. 377.)

The appeal of the tragedies of the past seems to be partly that they are past. Lacking the distancing effect of time, the modern would-be tragedian was required, therefore, to employ artistic devices to achieve the same distance – to veil the existence of evil in a poetic form, rather than depicting sordid and vulgar facts in painful detail.

In contrast, there were growing numbers of critics prepared to defend the new tragic novels precisely for their realism, and for the absence of any distancing or ennobling formal beauty. James's *The Wings of the Dove*, for instance, was

> not like a great tragedy of the older kind, which ends in some ennobling resolution of error through death. It ends in a deep, resonant discord. But

such a discord equally has its place in art, for it might actually close just such a passage of significant, tumultuous life.   (Oliver Elton, 'The Novels of Mr. Henry James', *Quarterly Review*, 198, 1903, p. 378.)

The cathartic resolution was rejected because it alleviated the horror of the tragic experience. Of *Rhoda Fleming*, W.E. Henley wrote, 'as the spectacle of a ruined and broken life is infinitely more discomforting than that of a noble death, I take it that Mr. Meredith was right to prefer his present ending to the alternative'.[14] The suggestion that it was life, not death, that is tragic, was particularly important and will be a major theme throughout this study. Henley's emphasis on the 'discomforting' element also implied that his judgement was more moral than aesthetic, whereas the classicist's reference was increasingly to a formal concept, as we have seen.

And yet those novelists attempting to create realistic tragedy did not altogether reject the classical model. In many cases they were trying to bring closer together traditional formal concepts of tragedy and contemporary tragic experience, the stylised and the real, the form and the feeling. Following the aims of traditional tragedy and, in some cases more precise aspects of form and structure, these novelists stressed the need for different subjects for contemporary versions of tragedy which could perhaps only be expressed through narrative forms, and yet could alone continue the spirit of tragedy. It is for this reason, for instance, that pathetic elements play such a vital role in the Victorian tragic novel. Pathos is not a negative effect, a token of a failure to achieve tragedy, but the result of a deliberate emphasis on passivity, helplessness and dull monotony by novelists concerned with working these concepts into a total and new version of tragedy.

In contrast, the many pastiches of Jacobean tragedy written at the beginning of the nineteenth century followed the style and content of the originals so closely that all sense of tragic immediacy was lost. G.H. Lewes referred to a conviction current among his contemporaries that their age and its habits were unfit for tragedy, 'the process of civilisation having softened down the violent contrasts of character, and the habits and customs of the age being less favourable both to heroic adventure and great tragic crimes'.[16] He argued that 'precisely because the passions are more subtle but less obvious, are they undramatic, and are fitted only for the novel, or for lyric and narrative poetry'. In order to convey the tragedy of contemporary life, the writer had to abandon the idea of poetic or ideal tragic drama for that of prosaic tragedy. The mean and petty aspects of modern life did not need to be concealed, for they added to the reality and pathos. Rejecting the idea that the age provided inappropriate material for tragedy, Lewes instead rejected the old forms, as inappropriate media for whatever tragedy existed in modern life. Rather than being antipathetic to tragedy, the novel was essential to its continuing existence and development.

Each critic's attitude to these two literary forms and the relationship between them depended on the place he assigned the novel in the literary tradition. Some saw the novel as the youngest part of a tradition that thrived on interconnections, and that its strength lay in its eclecticism. But others saw the novel standing apart, divorced from the wider tradition by its basis of realism, that is, as a 'life-form', rather than an 'art-form'. The novel's defenders acknowledged the historical gulf between the novel and the other literary forms, but saw literary history simply as an explanation for the link between drama and the tragic vision, rather than proof of its inevitability, or as a reason for dissociating the novel from the traditional concerns of serious literature. They concluded that, if Shakespeare were alive in Victorian England, he would write novels.

It is with the arguments of the latter group of critics that this study will mainly be concerned, although the doubts raised by their opponents have to be considered. And there are problems raised by neither group. Those who suggested that the novel could do much, if not all, that tragic drama did, rarely suggested exactly how this was to be done, given the acknowledged differences between the two forms. But their most valuable contribution is the suggestion that some of the finest work of the period resulted from a balanced interplay between the novel and tragedy, the tension between the realistic bias of the novel and the dramatised, idealised principles of tragic drama. They saw, and welcomed, a union of two apparently opposing tendencies – the universal and elemental aspects of tragedy with the contemporary realities of the novel.

I

THE TRAGIC PHILOSOPHY:
DETERMINISM AND FREE WILL

The tragic view of life affirms both the inevitability of suffering and evil, and their irrelevance. It gives a bleak picture of human life, but remains positive because it simultaneously affirms a faith in human goodness. That this goodness may be unavailing is but a testimony to the courage of those who have faith in it. The strength of the moral lesson is untouched: virtue is its own reward. If tragedy so often ends with the restoration of order, this is not the direct result of good so much as a symbolic vindication of its existence. To explain the continual presence of evil and suffering in deterministic terms may seem to leave no room for free will, and therefore for any meaningful individual virtue. Those theories variously described as 'deterministic', 'fatalistic' or 'necessitarian' might appear incompatible with a tragic philosophy. And yet the clash which is found in the work of so many Victorian novelists, between deterministic forces or 'Necessity' and the individual's will, has a philosophical basis which is the crux of tragedy.

(i) VARIETIES OF DETERMINISM

George Eliot's concept of determinism is, like that of Henry James, not of a system of abstract forces, but of a system of human relationships – private and public. The system, is, therefore, the cumulative result of individual wills, athough it is so complex that it appears to be beyond human control. Her use of the web image in her portrait of provincial society, *Middlemarch* (1871–2), suggests that society is a network which responds throughout to the slightest movement in one part. Hardy places less emphasis on these social relationships than on 'social machinery' – those laws and institutions which so often express man's inhumanity to man. In these institutions, society codifies its morality. And in his work we are as aware of the physical as the human environment. The tragedy is completed by the system of Nature or 'Necessity', expressed both in the environment and as an overwhelming biological force which drives the individual into conflict with society. The social reflects a universal condition.

George Eliot

Even before his birth, the individual's fate is shaped by the past through the intimate process of heredity. Then his family imposes inescapable obligations, traditions and restrictions upon him. *The Spanish Gypsy* (1868) gives great weight to the principle of heredity, which seems appropriate to the symbolic nature of the poetic drama. But it is otherwise a small, and not always satisfactory element in George Eliot's vision. The realism of her novels is disturbed by the melodramatic intrusion of the heredity principle. A public quarrel in *Felix Holt* (1866), between Harold Transome, proud heir to the Transome estates, and Jermyn, the sharp family lawyer he despises, leads to the revelation in a mirror of a likeness which confirms that Harold is Jermyn's son. Harold has already effectively proved himself to be Jermyn's son by his behaviour; this stress on the biological link is an unnecessary addition. The pressures that the family exert are far more convincingly portrayed. Whether through a conscious sense of obligation, or because 'Nature, that great tragic dramatist,. . .ties us by our heart-strings to the beings that jar us at every movement,'[1] the individual is rarely able to choose his path freely. The predicament is most acute when the influence of the family is in conflict with the influence of education, duty and affection with self-fulfilment. Maggie Tulliver's reading and the friendship of the artistic Philip Wakem reinforce the demands of her imagination and her instinctive revolt against the straitened conventionality of her mother's family, the Dodsons, and the drab world of *The Mill on the Floss* (1860). In such a case, no choice can be free; no choice can be satisfactory.

There are less intimate pressures on the individual, for – in one of George Eliot's most quoted statements – 'there is no private life which has not been determined by a wider public life'.[2] Every character has an occupation or public persona which affects all aspects of his life. In *Adam Bede* (1859), the carpenter hero finds satisfaction and fulfilment in the craft which offers full rein for his abilities, and reasonable independence. But Tertius Lydgate, the talented young doctor who comes to Middlemarch in the hope of also carrying out his scientific research, finds his pioneering methods unpopular not only with the rest of his profession, but with public opinion, including that of his wife. His desire to retain his professional and moral integrity is further weakened by the power of money, which affects all other relationships. Even the Reverend Camden Farebrother, a generous and honourable man, is led – because of an income insufficient to support his aunt, mother and sister – into gambling, so winning the disapproval of enemies and friends. Lydgate has to learn, as Farebrother did, that 'it's rather a strong check to one's self-complacency to find how much of one's right doing depends on not being in want of money'.[3]

The difference between Adam Bede and Lydgate, as far as their work is concerned, is partly due to the changed social setting, the greater modernity of *Middlemarch*. The later novel shows a society beset by historical, political and social changes, 'constantly shifting the boundaries of social intercourse, and begetting new consciousness of interdependence' (I, p. 142). The old organic community of Hayslope has been replaced by a far more complex, unstable world where the status and wisdom of the professional and upper classes are no longer held as god-given and unquestionable. Professional ability is not enough; uniformity with the patterns of social intercourse is vital. The doctor must bow to the power of Rumour, the voice of the community at its most hostile.

Henry James

James's vision of life shows similarities with George Eliot's which make him, rather than Hardy, her literary successor. In his work the 'bond of blood' everywhere exercises its stranglehold. Kate Croy, the villainous beauty who, with her reluctant fiancé, Merton Densher, tricks Milly Theale, the dying heiress of *The Wings of the Dove* (1902), has had her life reduced to 'mere inexhaustible sisterhood'[4] by the demands of her family. And although the parents of many of his central characters are dead, James's juxtaposition of past and present emphasises the influence of the 'dead hand' which George Eliot shows exercising so strong and withering a grasp on the living.

Without laying too heavy a stress on heredity, James gives sufficient indication of the quality his characters share with their parents to suggest his awareness of this factor. Isabel Archer, the heiress of *The Portrait of a Lady* (1881), is the imaginative and slightly reckless daughter of an improvident father with a taste for doing things on a grand scale, just as Rowland Mallett, in James's first novel, *Roderick Hudson* (1875), is very much the son of his gentle Dutch mother. But James's main emphasis is on the educative rather than biological influence. The upbringing of Pansy Osmond, Isabel's step-daughter, is a poignant example. Not only is her life shaped by her authoritarian father, but she must also conform to the régime of the convent, an image of the rigid environment. James frequently interrupts the chronological narrative of a novel to provide a detailed biography of one of his characters. He ensures that the reader has the information necessary to perceive the major influences on the individual, and relate them to subsequent, usually consequent, developments.

Beyond this insidious set of familial influences lie powerful social pressures. Unlike George Eliot's characters, James's are often free from the pressure of work, but they are all affected by the most influential factor in the society he portrays – money. Both the absence of money and its surfeit create their own pressures. Poverty prevents Kate Croy and Merton Densher from marrying, and gives them a motive – if not an excuse – for taking advantage of Milly. Wealth makes Milly, like Isabel Archer, the inevitable prey of fortune-hunters.

Money creates false relationships, in which human beings destroy each other for the financial benefits of marriages, deeds and wills. The social system is based on market values and market morality: 'nobody here does anything for nothing.'⁵ Personal relationships are absorbed into the system. A child, a wife, a sister, is a valuable, not an invaluable, asset: Gilbert Osmond literally sets a great price on his daughter. And the exclusiveness of this wealthy society imposes the burden of a public persona on the private individual. In *The American* (1877), Claire de Cintré finds the demands of this world doubly acute. She is forced to leave the man she loves, entering a convent instead, because her family expect her not only to consolidate the failing family fortunes, but to satisfy the family honour. Her 'American' is a self-made man, obtaining his wealth from vulgar commerce. The family's requirements are unlikely to be satisfied by one man in the changing world James portrays.

But the emphasis James gives to what is thwarted by these pressures is different from George Eliot's. In several of his major novels, the central character is a rich orphan. Free of family and financial pressures, what obstacles can there be to his or her fulfilment? Such characters are not simply prevented from achieving their desires, as George Eliot's are. They are prevented from forming those desires in freedom. The young individual has not even reached the point at which George Eliot's begin. For James, it is the more fundamental thwarting of the individual's identity, not his achievement, that is most tragic. James is equally capable of rendering the tragedy of maturity, as is evident from a novel like *The American*, which deals with the love-affair of two mature people. But his tragedies of youth stress the danger of the individual becoming the artefact. Forces beyond the individual's control make many of his decisions for him, before he is aware of a choice to be made. The fight to retain his integrity and identity is at the root of every character's ambitions.

The final tragic paradox is that, in trying to resist the particular pressures of which he is aware, the individual may find himself unconsciously subject to many more. Identity is liable to shift with each change of scene or situation; character become unstable, choices haphazard and out of keeping with the individual's true needs. Kate Croy is determined to be free, both from her lover's demands that she accept him and poverty, and from her rich aunt's that she accept her choice of husband with her wealth. She therefore maintains a dual identity – one for the world at large, and a secret one for Densher. She is able to 'cut her connexions and lose her identity.'[6] But her chosen rootlessness makes her lose all sense of what is due to her moral self, her integrity. She has consistency of purpose, but not of morality. Constantly surprising those around her with her unpredictability, her relationships are inevitably precarious. Isabel Archer is similarly exposed to the dangers of rootlessness, but is warned by the example of Madame Merle: 'Isabel found it difficult to think of her in any detachment or privacy, she existed only in her relations, direct or indirect, with her fellow-mortals.'[7]

Thomas Hardy

In Hardy's view, 'tragedy may be created by an opposing environment either of things inherent in the universe, or of human institutions'.[8] In his novels, it is often created by a conflict not simply between the individual and the environment, but between 'things inherent' and 'human institutions', a conflict at the individual's expense. His tragedies often arise out of the social situation: situations such as he described in his article, 'The Dorsetshire Labourer' (1883).[9] But the social is involved in so

complex a relationship with the 'things inherent' that the temporary, contingent elements themselves seem in many ways immut-
able.

The physical elements of climate and countryside, as the most
obvious 'things inherent in the universe', are an important plot-
ting device in Hardy's novels, where they so often defeat the
individual's efforts. In *The Mayor of Casterbridge* (1886), the
'god of the weather' and the uncertainties of the harvest hasten
Michael Henchard's fall from Mayor to bankrupt, as they likewise
favour the rise of his rival, Donald Farfrae. Believing in the
'weather-prophet' Fell's ability to predict the weather, Henchard
buys up grain in the expectation of a ruined harvest and high
prices, but is forced to sell it off cheaply when fine weather
pushes prices down, only to find the arrival of the predicted bad
weather raises prices again. Farfrae is able to profit from these
fluctuations because he acts cautiously, *after* the event, rather than
assuming he can control it.

But it is less easy to control those things inherent in man. Farfrae's success is greatly helped by the legendary 'canniness' of the
Scot. Heredity plays a more powerful role than it does in the
work of George Eliot or Henry James. It is less incongruous in
the more primitive world of rural Wessex.

> I am the family face;
> Flesh perishes, I live on,
> Projecting trait and trace
> Through time to times anon. . .
> The eternal thing in man,
> That heeds no call to die.
>
> (*Collected Poems*, 1919, p. 408.)

When the heroine of *Tess of the D'Urbervilles* (1891) kills her
seducer, Alec D'Urberville, Hardy describes the act as 'the hereditary quality';[10] Tess's crime is another such as her ancient family
had doubtless been guilty of – an aberration in that decadent
blood – just as her seduction had been a reversal of the seduction
of young peasant girls by her aristocratic ancestors. There are
important, more immediate factors, but by relating Tess's ex-

perience to the past, Hardy absorbs her personal situation into a vast system of causation.

Inherent in almost all Hardy's characters are those natural instincts which become destructive because social convention either suppresses or stultifies them, attempting to make the spirit conform to the 'letter'. *Jude the Obscure* (1895) concerns two cousins – Jude Fawley and Sue Bridehead – who start out with the handicap of an inherited passion for learning and a family tradition of disastrous marriages. This inheritance acts as the tragic 'flaw' because the desire for learning brings Jude into conflict with a social and educational system which cannot cater for the needs of a youth of his class or individuality. And he is forced into a marriage which incurs the family fate – like the curse that hangs over the House of Atreus in the Aeschylean trilogy – because his sexual instincts lead him into the arms of the unscrupulous Arabella Donne, and his instinctive honesty cannot allow him to escape the trap she has set for him. This conflict between sex and marriage is a conflict between the feelings of the moment and an institution which lasts a lifetime. It is the most recurrent illustration in Hardy's novels of the conflict between 'things inherent' and 'human institutions'. This is the 'tragedy of marriage, full of crimes and catastrophes', and ending only 'with the death of one of the actors'.[11]

Nor are social pressures confined to those urban areas where society's hierarchies are most in evidence, as *The Return of the Native* (1878) shows. Clym Yeobright, the 'Native', tires of city life and leaves Paris for the countryside of his youth, in the hope of escaping from such pressures in this isolated rural society. But he is disappointed. The public persona is equally important here, in this strongly conservative world. Clym's ambitions to teach the labourers are ridiculed because they threaten the existing social structure – such work is beneath him, and may give the labourers ideas above their station. Any deviation from the norms of society will be punished by society.

For society operates the final sanction of economic pressure.

Even those who withstand social contempt and isolation succumb to financial need. The threat of poverty sends young Tess Durbeyfield into the home of strangers, spuriously connected to her family by name, where she is seduced by Alec D'Urberville, the young master. And although she resolutely refuses help from him when she becomes pregnant, she is later forced back into his protection by her family's destitution. This economic insecurity is exacerbated by social forces totally beyond the control of those most vulnerable to them. The realities of eviction, the annual migrations in search of labour, and the changing relationship between tenant and farmer, all play their part in the fortunes of Hardy's characters. But few will listen to the plea of men like Jude: 'it was my poverty and not my will that consented to be beaten' (*Jude the Obscure*, p. 393).

Education, which seems to offer escape from this economic insecurity, only fosters dissatisfaction with the existing way of life. Tess, dreaming of becoming a teacher, and Jude, dreaming of the spires of Christminster, both learn this to their cost, trapped in their historical situation. Clym's education is ultimately a burden, because although he is a product of his education, he is equally a product of the heath, and longs for a simple life in communion with this natural world. His wife Eustacia's education makes this same heath her 'Hades', because of the contrast between the world of books and the world of Rainbarrow. The conflict is, like that experienced by many of George Eliot's characters, a conflict between the educated response and the familiar.

Education, in fact, seems to have little positive impact on Hardy's rural community, particularly on the philosophy of its inhabitants. They remain, on the whole, fatalistic. And their fatalism contributes to their tragedy; it is itself the product of heredity and circumstance, and in turn makes the individual submit to these and other forces. Hardy's vision of life has a deterministic basis similar to that of George Eliot and Henry James, but it is expressed as fatalism to convey the experience of his characters. His vision seems, therefore, dependent more on concepts of Fate and Nature than on those social elements which are equally, if not more, important to him.

Even the Christianity which the community professes is a mere veneer for a more deeply-rooted paganism. Evidence of their superstition is shown in *The Woodlanders* (1887), where the young girls of Hintock carry out an ancient ritual on old Midsummer Eve in the hope of a glimpse of their future marriage-partners.

Joan Durbeyfield may associate 'Nater' with 'what do please God', but her belief in the inevitability of her daughter's seduction has little to do with the Church which refuses a Christian burial to Sorrow, 'the gift of God', the offspring of that seduction. The confusion of language reflects the confusion of thought. Pagan superstition is oddly reinforced by the concepts of right and wrong, and of a final judgement, absorbed from Christianity. These country men are convinced of the existence of Necessity, experience verifying the idea that no one can escape the past.

The concept of Fate seems to be contradicted by the idea of Chance, so recurrent a motif in Hardy's fiction. But his novels show Chance conforming to a pattern, taking on the 'air of design' which Aristotle felt made the best kind of tragic plot (*Poetics*, IX). Tess is repeatedly faced with the wrong man: as a maiden she is doomed to be seen and desired by Alec D'Urberville, while Angel Clare who sees and loves her does so when it is too late. When she confesses her relationship with Alec to Angel, her behaviour would have won round any man but Angel – the only man she needs to win round. Sexual encounters are inevitably ill-fated, not because the right partners do not exist, but because 'the man to love rarely coincides with the hour for loving' (*Tess of the D'Urbervilles*, p. 49).

Chance is particularly likely to fall into such nightmarish patterns for those who are prone to superstition. Belief in omens tips the scales in favour of their being fulfilled: it diminishes the ability to choose freely. The relationship between the omen and later events begins to look more than coincidental, if not yet causal. For the omen is often archetypal, representing probability, because it (the archetype) portrays ordinary instinctive events as types.

The idea of Chance, then, only reminds the reader of the sphere of ideal possibilities, of what ought to be happening but is not. The illusion of freedom diminishes in the course of Hardy's novels. The net narrows and finally closes. All the main characters of his tragic novels seem, as he suggested of Tess and Angel, under *any* circumstances doomed to unhappiness. Even the most improbable coincidences are merely accelerating factors. Given the principle of heredity, the character and environment of the protagonists, the outcome is inevitable. Heredity and environment, character and society, are each conceived as modern Fates. Primitive superstition and scientific theory reinforce each other. Whether we call this vision 'fatalistic' or 'deterministic' is of relatively minor importance.

(ii) 'CHARACTER IS FATE': DEGREES OF FREEDOM

The much-discussed quotation from Novalis appears in both George Eliot's and Hardy's work, providing the key to the philosophy they share with James. Its ambivalence, which has given rise to so many contradictory interpretations, is the basis of the tragic paradox, reconciling the concept of determinism with free will. It is not a question of deciding whether character is predestined, or conversely that character determines destiny; each is equally true. Novalis's words, literally translated, were 'Fate and Character are but names for one idea.' Determined by heredity and environment, character in turn interacts with environment to work out the individual's destiny. Character alone rarely determines destiny. If Michael Henchard is a 'man of character', it is only because his character aids and abets those forces which destroy him. But character does play its part, explaining why the determining forces already discussed do not affect all people equally, why poverty, for instance, does not drive all to either ruin or dishonesty. What differs in the work of the three novelists is the balance of power within the character-fate relationship.

George Eliot stresses the vulnerability of character, the need to cultivate strength of will. 'Character is not cut in marble – it is not something solid and unalterable. It is something living and changing, and may become diseased as our bodies do' (*Middlemarch*, III, p. 310). In *Adam Bede*, a complex series of image-patterns suggests that character may itself be a determining factor. Adam has the strength of the wood of his trade; Hetty is associated with the shifting medium of water, in which – after murdering her illegitimate child by Arthur Donnithorne – she half-heartedly attempts to drown herself. But to underline her conviction that character is not static, but constantly exposed to temptation, the novelist introduces a further distinction, discriminating between the unbending oak of the carpenter, and the willow, bent by the attraction of water. It is beside a willow tree that the dead body of Adam's drunken father is found, and it is by the Willow Brook that Hetty appears in Adam's dream.

Both George Eliot and Henry James distinguish between innate characteristics and what, at its most trivial, can be called mere habit. It is all too easy to become a 'deeds-creature', like the heroes of Jacobean tragedy. Once a wrongful act has been committed, choosing the right becomes harder. Circumstances make such a choice increasingly difficult and egotism becomes ingrained. The link with the Shakespearean concept of the tragic character is evident. We are reminded of Macbeth,

> . . .in blood
> Stept in so far that, should [he] wade no more,
> Returning were as tedious as go o'er.
> (*Macbeth*, III, iv, ll.136–8)

Each individual must establish a moral tradition as protection from temptation. Arthur Donnithorne's seduction of Hetty Sorrel leads him into a deceitful baseness totally out of character in the good-natured fellow he considers himself to be. He assumes he is incapable of harm because he has never been tested. As there is no precedent of self-sacrifice, he continues to do as he pleases even when this hurts others.

James shows Christina Light, the heroine of *Roderick Hudson*, attempting to reverse this process. Having behaved badly in the past, under the corrupt influence of her mother, she wishes to create a new moral tradition, to live up to a stranger's – Rowland Mallet's – idea of her capabilities. She seeks a course of action which will create a new identity for herself, hoping to escape from her past and the self with which she is so bored. But her failure suggests that James believes more in the power of circumstances and habit than in the will to freedom.

How far, in fact, can any act be free, and how effective can it be? No action is free in the sense that it is uncaused, but if the individual is aware of such causes, he can attempt to resist his own baser motives. He can act rationally, rather than irrationally. For a cause is not a compulsion. Whoever continually blames his environment for his failures is providing excuses rather than ex-planations; the environment is likely to be a cause, but it is no com-pulsion. As George Eliot puts it, 'it always remains true that if we had been greater, circumstance would have been less strong against us' (*Middlemarch*, III, p. 82). Some give way when tested, others do not. In *Daniel Deronda* (1876), the prospect of poverty for herself and her family induces Gwendolen Harleth to marry Grandcourt, even though her knowledge of his discarded mistress and illegitimate son appals her. But the honesty of Middle-march's Mary Garth makes her refuse the dying Peter Feather-stone's request that she burn his second will, even though she has reason to believe that this may secure an inheritance for the man she loves. Michael Henchard is destroyed by the economic and social upsets that befall him; but in *Far from the Madding Crowd* (1874), although totally deprived of his livelihood when a young sheep-dog drives his flock over a cliff, Farmer Oak survives to achieve wealth and happiness. He has that strength of character which knows when to submit to the inevitable, rather than in-stinctively fighting circumstances.

To suggest the degree to which character is involved in tragedy, Henry James shows that circumstances can be seen as opportunities. The visit to Europe which exposes Roderick Hudson to such dangerous seductive circumstances – the proverbial wine, women and song – is intended to be a great educational opportunity for the young artist. His fiancée, Mary Garland, experiences it as such, even though the visit robs her of Roderick: it widens her horizons and develops her moral and aesthetic sense. Although fearing the break with the past, she retains her integrity, taking from Italy only what she needs – only what she believes is valuable to her future as Roderick's wife. Opportunities become circumstances only when the will fails. It is only because Isabel Archer is afraid of the responsibility of using her unlimited opportunities wisely that she becomes trapped in a difficult marriage. She abdicates her choice, offering her opportunities, with herself, to Gilbert Osmond. If external factors determine the individual's life, it is at least partly through his own complicity.

The individual, then, acts neither in isolation nor in ways that can be explained wholly by circumstance. The conflict is within as much as without the individual. It lies in what George Eliot calls 'that partial, divided action of our nature which makes half the tragedy of the human lot' (*The Mill on the Floss*, II, p. 370). The insight conveyed by her ironic phrase, 'the circumstance called Rosamond' (*Middlemarch*, II, p. 109) is shared by James. Both recognise that the insidious influence of the outside world is such that the individual shall to some degree love the world he wishes to reject. They recognise that circumstances merely develop and bring into action latent tendencies, usually the worse, rather than better, half of the divided self.

What George Eliot and James see as a choice between rational and irrational action, Hardy – in *The Dynasts* (1903–8) – expresses as a choice between acting according to those impulses we call instinct or according to those feelings derived from the world about us – demands that the individual take into account the 'other', not only the self. But in the novels, the emphasis is more

often on the conflict between the individual and the outside world
than on that within himself, so that the conflict seems unequal,
and the element of choice more theoretical than real. Hardy is
usually less concerned than George Eliot and James with the
formation and development of character, with the effect of environment on what a man is, than with its effect on what he does.
And the distinction between what he is and does if often tragic.
Circumstances prevent the individual from translating what he is
and aspires to into action. The freedom of thought and feeling
impresses itself on the reader less than the absence of free action.
This theoretical freedom seems so abstract as to be almost negli-
gible.

If freedom exists at all, for Hardy it is to be found in knowledge. Only by learning that we are less free than we thought, can
we learn to become more free. Henry James also sees freedom as
being allied to knowledge. By accepting the inevitable, the individual may be released from ineffectual desires, seeking instead to
master the inner life, to seek progress in terms of consciousness,
rather than achievement. By realising that Milly Theale's 'caged
freedom' (*The Wings of the Dove*, II, p. 150) is the only kind
there is, he can learn to make good use of the space within the
cage, not to clutter it up with inessentials. He can learn to accommodate his desires to his own limitations and external limits.
But James sees this renunciation of illusion in terms of forfeiture,
and Hardy's attitude to knowledge is ambiguous. If knowledge
leads not to escape, but only to a greater certainty of the limits of
the cage, then it seems a doubtful blessing. Life is

> A senseless school, where we must give
> Our lives that we may learn to live!
> ('A Young Man's Epigram on Existence', *Collected Poems*, p. 281.)

We suffer in order to learn, but learn only that we must suffer.
This is the 'ingenious machinery contrived by the Gods for reducing human possibilities of amelioration to the minimum –
which arranges that wisdom to do shall come *pari passu* with the

[margin: illusion of freedom]

departure of the zest for doing' (*The Mayor of Casterbridge*, p. 369).

George Eliot arrives at a more positive conclusion. She, too, stresses the need for knowledge: forewarned is forearmed. With foresight, will can overcome desire. For 'we prepare ourselves for sudden deeds by the reiterated choice of good or evil which gradually determines character'.[12] Rational choice is, in turn, the product of experience, and only the consistent experience of cause and effect that a deterministic universe produces can lead to truly moral choice, a choice which is based on what experience has shown to be right, both in itself and in its consequences. Knowledge and, consequently, freedom are only made meaningful by a deterministic structure such as George Eliot envisages.

Armed with knowledge of themselves and the world, George Eliot's heroes are able to distinguish what can be altered from what must be accepted. They concentrate their energy on the battles that can be won, beginning with the conflict within themselves. They possess what Wordsworth called a 'wise passiveness', shared by Hardy's countrymen – in particular, Gabriel Oak, whose very name reminds us of George Eliot's carpenter hero, and Michael Henchard's long-suffering step-daughter, Elizabeth-Jane. Hardy rejects total passivity, as it is the commonest cause of tragedy:

A Plot, or Tragedy, should arise from the gradual closing in of a situation that comes of ordinary human passions, prejudices, and ambitions, by reason of the characters taking no trouble to ward off the disastrous events produced by the said passions, prejudices and ambitions.
  (F.E. Hardy, *The Early Life of Thomas Hardy 1840–91*, 1928, p. 157.)

But in Michael Henchard, constantly defying weather, society and his own more generous impulses, Hardy reminds us of the Shakespearean tragedy of will. Such over-reaching quickly becomes the classical *hubris*. What is required is that gentle, yet dogged, persistence which develops the potential of a man's destiny to the full, without exceeding its limits. But the knowledge Hardy's heroes acquire more often leads to desperate impotence than meaningful action. The 'minute forms of satisfaction' which Elizabeth-Jane clings to seem almost totally negative when compared with the individual's original hopes.

Henry James also rejects aggressive wilfulness because it can only be exercised at the expense of his 'free spirits'. The will is strongest and finest when its two elements – intent and desire, the rational and passionate motives – are united. When they conflict, they become a source of weakness. Roderick Hudson's artistic ambition begins as a passionate ideal, but degenerates into a merely intellectual idea, divorced from and subordinate to the more prosaic desires engendered by Europe. In contrast, in such moments of crisis as Milly's death, Merton Densher's answer in *The Wings of the Dove* is to do nothing: 'to create the minimum of vibration' (ii, 226). But the free spirit should not abdicate from life so as to avoid suffering. In reaction to the loss of his wife, Dr Sloper of *Washington Square* (1880) deliberately stifles his feelings for his daughter, assuming an ironic, detached standpoint. To avoid the risk of again being hurt, he deprives himself of Catherine's love. In Jamesian terms, such characters are barely alive. Duty might seem to dictate the need for passivity and renunciation. And conscious acts of forfeiture such as Isabel Archer makes when she returns to her husband are morally positive in their alert acceptance of a hard-won truth. But James believes that 'there is in the human heart a sentiment higher than that of duty – the sentiment of freedom; and in the human imagination a force which respects nothing but what is divine'.[13] And yet, if freedom depends on recognising how little freedom exists, we are back at renunciation. James's novels, like Hardy's, leave the reader aware less of what is to be gained by knowledge and experience than of the sense of loss to which they lead.

(iii) TRAGIC RESPONSIBILITY

Without this tenuous element of freedom, however, the individual would be relieved of all responsibility for his actions and their consequences. Tragedy demands some kind of just relationship between the individual and his fate. He may be more sinned against than sinning, but, for his fate to be tragic, he must be at some stage actively and consciously involved in the course of events which initiates the disaster. None of the three novelists under discussion seeks to diminish either the individual's responsibility for his actions, or the power of the forces against him.

Determinism is not, as so many Victorian critics claimed it was, conducive to lax morals. For, in the final ethical analysis, the element of freedom becomes strangely irrelevant. Because the odds against her are so great, Tess remains innocent, 'a pure woman', although the mother of an illegitimate child, and a murderess. But, like Orestes, she has committed certain acts and must pay the price. And however small a degree of responsibility the individual bears for his actions, he must be aware of his responsibility to those affected by them. The emphasis each novelist gives to the past helps the reader to understand why a character acts as he does, but on the ethical plane the emphasis is on the future, on the need for looking forward. If a man's own life has been cruelly affected by the selfish or unthinking action of another, there is a good reason for him to ensure that those nearest to him shall not suffer as a result of his actions. The emphasis is as much on consequence as cause.

This is particularly true of George Eliot's novels, where the law of consequences governs the universe. Given the close network of human relationship, the consequences of each action are incalculable and irrevocable: 'anyone watching keenly the stealthy convergence of human lots, sees a slow preparation of effects from one life on another, which tells like a calculated irony on the indifference of the frozen stare with which we look at our unintroduced neighbour' (*Middlemarch*, 1, p. 142). The relationship between the individual and his environment is a two-way process. Just as Arthur Donnithorne is influenced by the idealised image which the community of Hayslope creates for him, so his private tragedy becomes a collective one when this community finds the

hopes invested in him shattered. A deterministic universe may
bring tragedy to the individual; it nevertheless demands a still
greater degree of responsibility on his part.

For he is responsible not only to his neighbour, but to the
human race. George Eliot and Hardy are meliorists, believing
that the progress of the world will only come about through the
actions of people as individuals. Even if ideals are unavailing in
practical terms, the ideals themselves, like feelings of sympathy,
contribute toward the future. As George Eliot's Dorothea Brooke
puts it, 'by desiring what is perfectly good, even when we don't
quite know what it is and cannot do what we would, we are part of
the divine power against evil – widening the skirts of light and
making the struggle with darkness narrower' (*Middlemarch*, 11,
p. 179). Compassion will follow when humanity perceives the
injustice and chaos that exists and realises that it is destroying
itself. For Hardy and George Eliot develop out of the pessimistic
materialism of Darwin's concept of Evolution a more optimistic,
moral theory. Where Darwin sees human progress as an accident
of organic evolution, George Eliot sees it as the product, further-
ing the primacy of love. For Hardy, too, evolution and love are
inseparable. Sympathy, because it entails a degree of self-
annulment, is a form of sacrifice, generated by our experiencing
the pain of others in ourselves. Self-sacrifice, therefore, is, in evolutionary terms, a form of self-preservation. In a cruel world, sympathy is more necessary than joy, so that the ideal of individuality
must be sacrificed to the ideal of the community. Indeed, the interests of both are seen to be one.

But, for Hardy and Henry James, this necessary sacrifice is
tragic – the outraged demands of the individual are never
silenced. In their novels the survival of the fittest is rarely the survival of the best. It is a commonplace of tragedy that the innocent
are least likely to be able to accommodate themselves to a world of
evil. But through the disproportionate suffering characteristic of
tragedy, the innocent make their own contribution. In his struggle
towards awareness, man makes a direct assault on evil, the

product of unconsciousness. He must, therefore, act as if he were free, even if he feels he is not. This is the only course of action which can be of any value.

By this act of faith, the individual achieves heroic stature. By clinging to the ideal even when overwhelmed by reality, he becomes an isolated representative of value. He is particularly isolated in the novels of Hardy and Henry James, where we find little or none of the mitigating Christian framework of George Eliot's novels. Dr Walter Lock of Keble called *Tess of the D'Urbervilles* 'the *Agamemnon* without the rest of the Oresteian trilogy'. To which Hardy responded, 'This is inexact, but suggestive as to how people think.'[14] It suggests, as do the allusions throughout his work to the Old Testament and Greek Tragedy, the sense of a rigid law, a law which must be adhered to not for the sake of happiness, but because it is the law, inexorable and inflexible.

Hardy, and to a lesser extent, James, see this law – natural or social – as being totally contrary to morality; George Eliot sees the law of consequences as a moral force. This distinction accounts for the more tragic tone of the male novelists, for George Eliot's characters are rarely faced with any gulf between morality and what we may generally term theology. Hardy and James, however, constantly assert the moral superiority of the individual over the workings of Necessity or society. Man has all the more responsibility for maintaining values because he finds them missing from his universe. As Hardy's 'God' muses:

> Forsooth, though I men's master be
> Theirs is the teaching mind!
>
> ('God's Education', *Collected Poems*, p. 262.)

2

FROM TRAGIC DRAMA TO THE
TRAGIC NOVEL

(i) THE DIVORCE BETWEEN TRAGEDY AND DRAMA

The decline of serious drama in Britain in the nineteenth century is a well-known phenomenon.[1] The relationship it bears to the corresponding rise of the novel is a problematic subject. Until the appearance of Shaw's plays at the end of the century, no contemporary drama of any stature or seriousness was produced in the theatre. It was not that tragedy or tragic themes were neglected, as they largely were in the eighteenth century, but works on tragic themes and subjects were written for private reading only. All the great nineteenth-century writers were poets or novelists, not dramatists. The separation from the live theatrical tradition, and the simultaneous development of the novel as a tragic form are surely not simply coincidental.

It is important to remember, of course, that while serious drama declined, the commercial theatre flourished, marking the increasingly significant division of literature into 'highbrow' and 'lowbrow'. It seemed that dramatists could no longer entertain as they taught, or *vice versa*. As the stage was more and more given over to melodrama, pantomime and even hippodrama – literally, horse-drama! – so more serious writers turned to the creation of what has become known as 'closet-drama'. The fact that such 'drama' was intended to be read rather than performed caused many contemporary critics to react as John Gibson Lockhart did, on reading Lord Byron's *Sardanapalus* (1821): 'in God's name, why call a thing a tragedy, unless it is meant to be a play?'[2] Closet-drama was, in addition, clearly intended for a literate élite, while the playwrights designed their work for a popular mass audience. The two strands which unite in great British drama – the literary, aesthetic principle, and the feeling for the contemporary and popular – were totally divorced. There could, therefore, be no great drama.

When we remember that almost all the great Romantic and Victorian poets attempted to write a poetic tragedy, for the 'closet', it may seem surprising that none of them produced anything that even approached real drama. But, as the Introduction suggested, their work was too often mere pastiche, reviving the style and themes of the drama of the past, rather than its spirit. Shakespeare was the commonest source of inspiration. His own *Shakespeare* plays were almost the only serious dramas to achieve popularity on the stage during this period. The fact that – as I also suggested in the Introduction – his work was rarely cited by critics as a model for tragedy is again indicative of the increasing gulf between popular and critical taste. This popularity undoubtedly relates to that interest in character which made Shakespeare such a positive source of inspiration for many of the great nineteenth-century novelists. But this stage success had disastrous consequences for the contemporary drama, which so carefully attempted to render the Shakespearean style. Augustin Filon complained, in his contemporary survey of nineteenth-century drama, that Shakespeare's spirit could not be assimilated: 'this is impossible to a man of our time: one can but dress oneself up in the cast-off garment which served as a cover to his genius. This garment does not suit us'. And by copying from the past, the dramatist lost sight of his own time, which it was his true function to reflect. As Filon put it, for contemporary drama to succeed, 'the choice has to be made between Shakespeare and life'.[3]

But Shakespeare was not the only model. Reviewing Matthew Arnold's *Merope* (1858), W.E. Henley objected that it was 'an imitation Greek play: an essay, that is, in a form which ceased long since to have any active life, so that the attempt to revive it – to create a soul under the ribs of very musty death – is a blunder alike in sentiment and in art'.[4] The would-be tragedians were imitating older literary forms, when the demand everywhere was for a living drama that modelled itself on nature. A living drama should express the ideas and passions of the age, and reflect the national character. Each age must therefore develop its own methods and language as a vehicle for these ideas.

In defence, Shelley claimed that it was precisely the inadequacy of the age that made it necessary for the dramatist to turn to the drama of the past.

> In periods of the decay of social life, the drama sympathises with that decay. Tragedy becomes a cold imitation of the form of the great master-pieces of antiquity, divested of all harmonious accompaniment of the kindred arts; and often the very form misunderstood, or a weak attempt to teach certain doctrines, which the writer considers as moral truths. (1821).   (*Shelley's Literary and Philosophical Criticism*, ed. by
> John Shawcross, 1909, p. 136.)

It was not the age that provided inadequate material for tragedy, but the old forms that were inadequate to convey the tragedy of the age.[5] For the ideas, passions and character of the age were finding expression in the novels of the period. This was perhaps the only place where they could find expression. As Henry James put it:

> The old dramatists. . .had a simpler civilisation to represent – societies in which the life of man was in action, in passion, in immediate and violent expression. Those things could be put upon the playhouse boards with comparatively little sacrifice of their completeness and their truth. Today we're so infinitely more reflective and complicated and diffuse that it makes all the difference. What can you do with a character, with an idea, with a feeling, between dinner and the suburban trains? You can give a gross, rough sketch of them, but how little you touch them, how bald you leave them! What crudity compared with what the novelist does!
> (*The Tragic Muse*, 2 vols., 1921, I, p. 59.)

James suggests that the novel penetrates the surface of modern life far better than drama can. And James's concern, like George Eliot's, was very much with the kind of tragedy which was not apparent on the surface. Until English translations of Ibsen's plays appeared in Britain towards the end of the century, many more critics claimed that realistic tragic drama was impossible. The heroism portrayed in many novels of modern life was essentially undramatic. In addition, the dramatist must constantly be making all processes of decision, all feelings, all communications, more articulate than they are in real life. If we want to see inarticulate people's decisions and experiences realistically portrayed, we must look to the novel, where direct speech can be amplified in narrative.

The novel obviously presented itself as a more satisfactory vehicle for modern tragedy than the drama had become. When serious drama was itself reduced to a form for private reading, the novel was a formidable rival. It combined its serious reflections on life with the popular appeal it shared with the theatre, healing – for a time – the breach between 'literature' and 'entertainment'. In the novel was also realised that ideal of interaction, of combining the dramatic and the narrative, the poetic and the contemporary reality, that critics of drama and the novel alike were demanding.

(ii) THE CLASSICAL INHERITANCE

In turning to the novel, and new versions of tragedy, writers did not, however, completely reject traditional tragic theory and practice. At a time when knowledge of the classics was far more widespread among the educated and literary than it is now, it is unlikely that any writer could form his ideas of tragedy in a void. Whether he imitated, modified or rejected the tradition, it is important to understand his feelings for, and relationship to, this classical inheritance.

George Eliot

Both Gordon Haight's biography of George Eliot and his edition of her letters show her thorough knowledge of classical literature.[6]

Early in her career as a novelist, she became well acquainted with the Greek tragedies, and she continued to refer to and re-read the plays throughout her life. She included Aristotle's *Poetics* in her reading, re-reading it in 1865, for instance, with renewed admiration. Although George Eliot admitted to only one classical quotation in all her novels – the *Philoctetes* quotation in 'The Sad Fortunes of the Reverend Amos Barton' (*Scenes of Clerical Life*, 1858) – other Greek quotations are used as headings to Chapters 42 and 48 of *Felix Holt*, and many more oblique references and allusions in her novels reveal that her knowledge of Greek tragedy was not simply a passive one.

The only explicit link between George Eliot's reading of the classics and her own writing can be found during the period of the conception of *The Spanish Gypsy*, her poetic drama, and *Felix Holt*. While writing *The Spanish Gypsy* in 1865, she read again Aeschylus and Kleist's *The Theatre of the Greeks*, hoping for inspiration. She describes the poem as being 'a little in the fashion of the elder dramatists, with whom I have perhaps more cousinship than with recent poets'.[7] At the time of writing *Felix Holt*, in 1866, she had also been reading Sophocles and the *Poetics*, and significantly refers to the 'later acts' of her novel.[8] The motto for Chapter 48 is her own, very personal interpretation of lines from Sophocles' *Ajax*:

> 'Tis law as steadfast as the throne of Zeus –
> Our days are heritors of days gone by. (II, 329)

Her translation gives emphasis to the doctrine of Nemesis, which she found so valuable in Aeschylus' work.

The relationship between *Felix Holt* and Greek tragedy has been discussed in some detail by F.C. Thomson, who argues that George Eliot meant the novel to conform to the example of Greek drama but fell short of her aim. In *Middlemarch*, however, 'George Eliot returned to the type of tragedy she had always understood so well and could give its proper form.'[9] While I would agree that *Felix Holt* is a less successful novel than *Middle-*

march, Thomson makes too rigid a distinction between the kind of tragedy to be found in *Felix Holt* and that found in George Eliot's other novels. The novelist frequently uses traditional tragic concepts such as *peripeteia* in her depiction of the clash between the individual and the inexorable law of consequences. But their significance lies in the way these concepts interact with George Eliot's vision of modern tragedy, to which they present a contrasting aesthetic and moral ideal. Even in *Felix Holt*, the 'modern' vision can be found in the pathetic tragedy of Mrs Transome, but the tension between the modern and traditional is not sustained as it is in her finest work, *Middlemarch* and *Daniel Deronda*.

Thomas Hardy

William Rutland's research in *Thomas Hardy: A Study of his Writings and their Background* (1938) suggests that Hardy's knowledge of the classics was less wide than George Eliot's. He was not taught Greek at school, although he began to learn Latin as an 'extra' at the age of twelve. But that he at some stage undertook a close study of the plays of Aeschylus and Sophocles is evident not only from the references and allusions to the tragedies in his novels, but from Hardy's own annotated editions of the Greek text, found at his home, Max Gate. It is not possible to give an exact date to the periods of Hardy's life when he studied the Greek masterpieces. But Hardy's second wife, in *The Early Life of Thomas Hardy*, tells us that Hardy taught himself Greek during the first few years of his apprenticeship as an architect, when he studied the *Agamemnon* and *Oedipus*. His friend Horace Moule, however, when asked by the novelist whether he should continue this study, advised against anything so totally unrelated to his career as an architect. Hardy's later reading of the dramatists was, therefore, of a more fragmentary nature, although his knowledge of them became substantial. There are certainly more references and direct debts to Greek tragedy in the later than in the earlier novels.

Among the more important of these allusions is the notorious translation from the *Prometheus Vinctus* at the end of *Tess of the D'Urbervilles* – the 'President of the Immortals' passage – and the allusion to the 'dramas of a grandeur and unity truly Sophoclean' that he depicts in *The Woodlanders* (1887) (p. 4). But evidence of Hardy's sympathy with the philosophy of the Greek tragedians is expressed not only by the omniscient narrator, but by the very action of his tragic novels. Above all he is influenced by Sophocles' vision of man as a plaything of malevolent gods, and by Aeschylus' stoical statement both of man's suffering and his greatness, summed up in the famous 'Aelinon, Aelinon!' of the *Agamemnon*, which Gilbert Murray translates as 'Sorrow, sing sorrow: but good prevail, prevail!'[10] Certain notebook entries Hardy made at the time of writing *Tess* illustrate his preoccupation with the Greek example. One note has obvious relevance to the novel:

When a married woman who has a lover kills her husband, she does not really wish to kill the husband; she wishes to kill the situation. Of course in Clytaemnestra's case it was not exactly so, since there was the added grievance of Iphigenia, which half-justified her.

(F.E. Hardy, *The Early Life of Thomas Hardy 1840–91*, 1928, p. 289.)

But Rutland's conclusions to the valuable research presented in his book are disappointing. His warning that Hardy was a modern, and therefore influenced as much by the intellectual thought of his own age as by that of the ancients, is a useful one. He fails to develop, however, his more interesting comment. He suggests that Hardy's relationship with the Greek classics was special, because he was 'as fully appreciative of the *form and technique* of Greek drama as of its intellectual and emotional significance' p. 40. More consistently and – I would argue – more successfully than George Eliot in *Felix Holt*, Hardy tries to create an analogue for this form of classical tragedy in the form of the novel. This is what finally sets him apart from George Eliot and Henry James.

Henry James

Leon Edel's biography of Henry James notes very few allusions to classical, or even neo-classical drama, and these occur in James's early life.[11] But references to contemporary dramatists like Ibsen are numerous (we must remember that James himself had ambitions to be a successful playwright). References to novelists, contemporary or past, are even more prolific. James appears to have little interest in tragedy as a literary form. But he uses the term constantly to express his view of human suffering: 'life is terrible, tragic, perverse and abysmal'.[12]

Tragedy appears to be for James, therefore, more a matter of material than of form. But in reading a novel like *The Portrait of a Lady*, the reader is aware not simply of the representation of tragic experience, but of certain formal qualities that recall classical tragic drama. Although it is not possible to establish direct links between James's aims and achievements, we can see a relationship between James's work and the theories and examples of classical tragedy. Daniel Lerner and Oscar Cargill have traced such a relationship between *The Bostonians* (1886) and the *Antigone*, and between *The Other House* (1896) and the *Medea*.[13] The most interesting aspect of this article is not so much that it establishes the classical background of these two specific novels – valuable as this is – as the demonstration that influences and analogies may be traced even in the absence of direct classical references. The authors suggest that James deliberately suppressed classical allusion in the bulk of his fiction, feeling it was inappropriate to the contemporary tone he wished to give his writing. But that the example of Greek tragedy should be assimilated almost unconsciously by a writer so concerned with tragic themes was inevitable.

(iii) TRAGEDY REDEFINED

The clash between the individual and the deterministic structure results in a dual movement of decline and regeneration. The tragic novels of George Eliot, Thomas Hardy and Henry James all retain this traditional pattern: the progression from egoism to altruism brought about by tragic suffering ensures that sacrifice is simultaneously salvation. Hardy's tragic novels also remain remarkably close to the tradition of tragedy in other respects, existing largely as stark outlines of events. In many aspects, therefore, they stand in contrast to the novels of George Eliot and James, who, in leading their reader's attention beyond the level of events, make the most radical attempts to redefine the nature of tragedy and of the heroism that accompanies it. Their more personal vision consists of an admiration for qualities which might seem essentially anti-heroic, and of an understanding of human suffering which gives real meaning to the phrase 'a fate worse than death'.

But Hardy introduces at least one new element into the traditional idea of tragedy. He uses working-class characters as material for tragedy – and far more successfully than George Eliot, because their tragedy arises, in part, out of their class, and he is not afraid to let their class experience, or the character, speak for itself. Hardy defends his concentration on the lower classes on aesthetic grounds. He claims that in tragedy social distinctions are unimportant, because 'education has as yet but little broken or modified the waves of human impulse on which deeds and words depend. So that in the portraiture of scenes in any way emotional or dramatic – the highest province of fiction – the peer and the peasant stand on much the same level'. If anything, social refinement stands in the way of the depiction of contemporary tragedy. It makes 'the exteriors of men their screen rather than their index'.[14] But, in extending the novel's range and shifting the focus of tragedy, Hardy is clearly involved with morality and society. His attempt to arouse the same pity and fear for the fates of his humbler characters that is traditionally experienced over the fates of noble leaders is no mere academic exercise.

George Eliot's theory of tragedy is based on an ideal of realism which links it with her theory of the novel. She believes that the

novelist's aim should be 'the extension of our sympathies'. This
can only be achieved by a realistic representation of that life of
which her largely middle-class readers hold false or unsympathetic
views. An idyllic portrait of the working-class merely reinforces the
reader's predilection for the picturesque or admirable, encouraging his ignorance and social apathy. George Eliot attacks Dickens
for failing to match his truthful delineation of idioms and manners with psychological truth, so that when passing on to an
emotional or tragic plane he becomes 'transcendent in his unreality', encouraging the 'miserable fallacy that high morality and
refined sentiment can grow out of harsh social conditions, ignorance and want'.[15] The situation most likely to arouse sympathy
for this alien reality is a tragic one, based as it is on the most
elemental forms of suffering. George Eliot's avowed method is
'to urge the human sanctities through tragedy – through pity and
terror as well as admiration and delights'.[16]

But if George Eliot's artistic and moral purposes can only be
achieved through tragedy, they also require the re-education of
her public, to whom her idea of tragedy is new. In her first work
of fiction, *Scenes of Clerical Life*, she constantly makes explicit
comparisons between her own vision of tragedy and the ideal
modes of contemporary fiction. This is not simply a defence of
her own fictional mode. Her ridicule of the literary tastes of
readers like 'Mrs Farthingale. . .to whom tragedy means ermine
tippets, adultery and murder'[17] is also an attack on their moral
sense. It is an attack on what she calls 'otherworldliness', on the
inability to associate heroism or tragedy with the contemporary
or familiar. George Eliot deplores this limited understanding of
human suffering and this blindness to real human dignity. She is
not merely a literary innovator, fusing tragic with realistic themes
and methods, but a moral teacher, awakening her readers to a
greater awareness of the sorrows and aspirations all around them.

Heroism is, for George Eliot, to be found in that 'wise passiveness' discussed earlier in Chapter 1 (p. 31). Her work does
not celebrate any heroic transgressions of the law, because she

[margin handwritten note: GE's view of the new tragedy]

accepts the morality of that inexorable law of consequence. The
nobly heroic is, in her eyes, inevitably tinged with egoism; it
disregards the reverberating complex of society. Like Henry
James, she is suspicious of the dramatic gesture, the act of sacrifice
so ostentatious that it defeats its own purpose. The heroine of
Romola (1863) is, at the beginning of the novel, a beautiful, noble
young Florentine, with a vision of a proud and heroic future. But
when the gradual knowledge of her husband Tito's baseness
forces her to abandon the ideal of her love, she finds – under the
influence of Savonarola – 'a new presentiment of the strength
there might be in submission'.[18] While Hardy shares George
Eliot's view of 'wise passiveness' as the safest course of action in
a deterministic universe, he does not see it as the heroic course.
If his heroes also display stoicism, it is the stoicism of endurance,
of passive resistance, rather than that of resignation and acceptance. Endurance is perhaps the greatest of the traditional tragic
virtues, as exemplified in Oedipus and King Lear. The endurance
of Hardy's characters often stems from that indignation which
W.B. Yeats calls 'a kind of joy', the joy that must accompany
tragic suffering.[19] George Eliot's heroes, in contrast, are educated
by their suffering into abandoning indignation, which she believes
is frequently mistaken for virtue. The modern world denies all
opportunity for such heroic action or outlets as were available to
a Saint Theresa in her time. It therefore creates both its own
forms of suffering and the need for new forms of heroism.

Because they adopt this attitude of resignation, George Eliot's
heroes rarely face the crises of traditional tragedy. But they do
not escape from tragic experience. Tragedy can arise from the
trivial as much as from the important events: 'it is in these acts
called trivialities that the seeds of joy are forever wasted, until
men and women look around with haggard faces at the devas-
tation their own waste has made'. George Eliot wishes to convey
'that element of tragedy which lies in the very fact of frequency'
(*Middlemarch*, II, p. 231 and I, p. 297). She suggests that such
monotonous daily suffering is as great a tragedy as (if not greater

Endurance

Resignation

than) death itself. Having sacrificed all egotistical hopes and desires, having ceased to live as an individual, it seems relatively easy to die in fact. George Eliot's novels suggest how superficial are our notions of tragedy, and question our habit of giving so central a place in it to death: 'It is a sad weakness in us, after all, that the thought of a man's death hallows him anew to us; as if life were not sacred too.' ('Janet's Repentance', *Scenes of Clerical Life*, ii, p. 176.) Her work anticipates Yeats's recognition that 'Only the dead can be forgiven' (*A Dialogue of Self and Soul*). It is again worth noting the contrast with Hardy, for whom it is death that gives life significance: 'the most prosaic man becomes a poem when you stand by his grave at his funeral and think of him'.[20] His attitude typifies the much more traditional concept of tragedy to which he adheres.

Henry James exploits the same preconceptions of heroism and tragedy as George Eliot, although far less explicitly. He presents both familiar and new versions of the tragic experience, so that the reader is forced to ask which relates most convincingly to his own experience. On the one hand there is the traditional tragic ending – the hero's death – and on the other the modern 'unfinished' ending – life goes on. In George Eliot's words, 'life must be taken up on a lower stage of expectation' (*Middlemarch*, iii, p. 181). Catherine Sloper of *Washington Square*, another victim of a fortune-hunter, Maurice Townsend, experiences this kind of finality to all her hopes and daydreams. After his return as a man who no longer has the power to move her in any way, she, picking up her embroidery, 'seated herself with it again – for life, as it were' (*Washington Square*, p. 234). In this case, there is no contrasted ending, and this is relevant to the form of the work as a whole.[21] But in *The Portrait of a Lady*, Isabel Archer's continuing life is set against her cousin Ralph Touchett's death; *Roderick Hudson* sets Rowland Mallett's future life against Roderick's death; and *The Wings of the Dove* sets Merton Densher's against Milly's. These juxtapositions suggest that death and life under such terms are very much the same thing. Discussing the idea of '*too late*' which is central to his concept of the unlived life, James states that 'the wasting of life is the implication of death'.[22] Death even seems a release compared with the daunting prospect of continuing without change, without hope, a life that has lost its motivation. On his deathbed, Ralph, at last able to show his love to Isabel, pities her because she has to go on living and suffering a loveless marriage.

But while James's concept of tragic suffering might seem close to George Eliot's, his concept of heroism is less like hers than might at first appear. Just as George Eliot's conception of heroism centres on resignation and duty, so James's novels offer apparently similar values in the form of renunciation and disinterestedness. But his 'renunciation' is a far less moral and more individualistic concept than George Eliot's 'resignation'. It is primarily a means to fulfilment and freedom, in favour of which James rejects duty. His heroes often refuse to commit themselves either to another individual or to any specific course of action, showing a desire for a more impersonal kind of fulfilment which renounces personal happiness. Such characters wish to avoid any involvement which will require them to take sides or compromise their freedom, which will corrupt their idealism into that morality known as 'being realistic'. In *The Spoils of Poynton* (1897) Fleda Vetch refuses to declare her affection for Mrs Gereth's son, Owen, or to give him any kind of encouragement, while he is still in any way attached to Mona Brigstock, in spite of her awareness of Owen's growing fondness for her, and Mrs Gereth's encouragement. Fleda will not commit herself to the man if this involves breaking her greater commitment to the ideal of acting unimpeachably. Fulfilment can only be measured in terms of such freedom. 'The free spirit, always much tormented and by no means always triumphant, is heroic, ironic, pathetic or whatever, and, as exemplified in the record of Fleda Vetch, for instance, "successful", only through having remained free.'[23] Moral value does not transcend the individual, as it does in George Eliot's novels. But James clearly shares that novelist's belief that it is far easier – as well as more irresponsible – to embark upon some heroic act of self- expression than to acquire the strength to remain passive. When Christina Light attempts to renounce Roderick Hudson for his own good, she is incapable of this kind of heroic self-effacement. She must make her act a dramatic gesture, and she thereby renders it ineffective.

The apparent negativity of the concepts of heroism of both George Eliot and James presents the novelists with difficulties. And these concepts are, of course, so essentially untheatrical as to be totally unsuited to drama. The successful outcome of the Jamesian quest for freedom is almost inevitably – in any practical sense – failure. The more the free spirit refuses to meddle with the lives of others, the more pathetic he is liable to appear in his inactivity. If renunciation and disinterestedness are heroic qualities, they are nevertheless in themselves not enough to turn James's energetic little spinster feminist, Miss Birdseye, into a heroine in the fictional sense. The individual must feel his sacrifice for it to be truly heroic. The heroic activity, as opposed to inactivity, lies in the mind which James shows assessing the picture. It is here, too, that the tragedy is wrought and intensified. In the living death with which he is concerned, unlike physical death, the consciousness survives, 'so that the man is the spectator of his own tragedy'.[24]

The sharper the individual's perceptions, the greater the irony of his inability to act upon them. Because he observes and understands the passing of his own unhappy life, his passivity is not pathetic, but tragic, offering as it does a comment on and explanation of the blind suffering of the helpless. James's heroes are able to transcend their involvement in their own situation, to see its wider relevance, because their consciousness turns naturally – through education and intellect – to analysis and abstraction. It is the relative rareness of such a consciousness that makes George Eliot's images of passive heroism – particularly among her working-class characters – pathetic rather than tragic.

3

REALISM AND TRAGEDY

Classical tragic drama not only does without, but requires the absence of, realism. As C.S. Lewis puts it: 'We do not know what anyone looked like, or wore, or ate. Everyone speaks in the same style.'[1] The realist's usual preoccupation with the details of everyday living appears irrelevant in a genre devoted to highlighting man's relationship with the Gods and with his fate. In the Victorian novel, the tragic mode had to come to terms with the methods of realism. For the Victorian novelist's interest in the individual's relationship with society is typical of what Raymond Williams calls the 'highest realism' – in which 'society is seen in fundamentally personal terms, and persons, through relationships, in fundamentally social terms'.[2] The writer who attempts to combine tragedy and realism has to find ways of isolating and universalising the individual's experience, to make him at once exceptional and representative, without destroying this sense that each element in society is inseparable from the whole. He has to endow mundane material with aesthetic and symbolic values without falsifying its nature.

The reality with which the Victorian novelist was generally concerned was, moreover, of a kind to appear particularly inappropriate to the traditional idea of tragedy. In their search for a mode of tragedy which would reflect the nature of their society, George Eliot, Thomas Hardy and Henry James often, therefore, modified this idea, as we saw in the previous chapter. All extended the areas of experience and society which could be considered suitable tragic subjects. The history of the novel itself, as it gradually supplanted drama as a popular literary form, marked a shift of interest from the great leader, with his actions of magnitude and his eloquence, to the more private experience of particular individuals, in an increasingly complex society. For the Victorian novelists, the focus was often even more specifically on the seemingly insignificant acts of the least powerful and articulate members of society. New conventions had, therefore, to be found to convey the traditional heroic and tragic values, if these values were not, indeed, to be changed altogether. Even for Henry James, concerned with a social élite, the problems raised by realism are remarkably similar to those faced by novelists portraying working-class life. For him, reticence, rather than inarticulacy is the key-word, but the issue remains the same – 'the grief that does not speak'.[3]

(i) 'THE OTHER SIDE OF SILENCE' – INARTICULACY AND DECORUM

If many of the characters of George Eliot and Hardy are un-exceptional in themselves, they become exceptional by virtue of their circumstances. The realism with which the novelists establish these circumstances is an essential aspect of their ability to interest the reader in the most ordinary of characters. In the early scenes of their novels, both writers create backgrounds in which the characters are established in some kind of normality. This normality is a world in which money counts, as it usually does in the world of prose. It counts for the most affluent of James's characters, and is even more painfully pervasive a concern in novels of working-class life. Tess Durbeyfield grows up in a home of 'unspeakable dreariness', the monotony and worry of which are only made bearable for her parents by the illicit trip to Rollivers, their 'local'. Here, as in the Hayslope of George Eliot's *Adam Bede*, is that close-knit rural community which seems to echo and magnify the individual's tragedy. The undesired intimacy of such environments can become intolerable to the sensitive. Through such mundane relationships a character's everyday reality is established as a basis for our understanding his behaviour under crisis.

Through the closeness of the relationship established between the character and his background, the novelist is also able to create a character who is both a hero and representative of his class – Aristotle's good but typical figure, the individual worthy to stand for his class. It is particularly difficult in working-class novels to reconcile the uniqueness of the individual with the quality of the type. How, for instance, can George Eliot give Adam Bede outstanding, heroic qualities and faithfully depict the life of his class without suggesting that only the exceptional, the déclassé, are admirable? She achieves this because, although constantly describing him as 'uncommon', as an above average man, she relates his best qualities to a simple family life of shared need and industry, which is seen as the most attractive aspect of working-class life. Adam's stature derives largely from the traditional strengths of the group he represents and upholds. His almost religious belief in work as a link with future generations reflects – it is implied – the working-man's ethic at its best. His sense of relationship is a refined development of the workman's solidarity and the peasant's sense of tradition and community. There are obviously idyllic elements in this conception, and George Eliot shows many examples of those who fail to live up to this ideal. But she insists that such exceptions exist in every generation, and relates the heroic elements to the class ethos here far more successfully than she does in *Felix Holt*, the story of another supposedly working-class hero, who seems to stand far outside, rather than for, his class.

Hardy's characters are similarly given both their representative and heroic qualities through their closest domestic and social relationships, and through their work. But his heroes often embody not so much the finest existing qualities of their class, as its potential, revealed in a sensitivity that implicitly or explicitly calls the reality into question. In contrast to her parents, Tess represents innocence burdened with the responsibility of careless neglect, almost replacing them as head of the family. In her relationships with other young girls, she displays an unusual power to evoke strong affection and loyalty which completely outweigh the usual sexual rivalry. This potential is not a desire to fulfil the ideals of the class, as in George Eliot, but a desire to escape it. Much as he regrets the passing of the traditional peasant life, Hardy is far more critical of its limitations than is George Eliot.

But our understanding of these characters does not derive simply from our knowledge of the external factors involved, but from our participation in their subjective experience. The concept of private tragedy depends very much on the private viewpoint. For an individual's inward suffering to impress the reader as tragic, the reader must share the utter exclusiveness of the experience for the individual, as well as seeing it in an inclusive, universal perspective such as symbolism may add. Hardy is aware that 'there's comedy in all things – when they don't concern you',[4] but he and George Eliot insist that the reader shall be concerned. They see that he shares the viewpoint of the individual who is to himself the centre of the universe. George Eliot, however, introduces alternative perspectives into the world of the novel itself, balancing the individual viewpoint of Dorothea Brooke, for instance, against that of her equally unhappy husband, Casaubon, rather than using symbol or image to suggest the universality of the main character's experience. She underplays the exclusiveness of the hero's experience in a way that places the tragic experience itself in perspective, as one element in the whole. This element of perspective is, inevitably, of considerable importance in differentiating the final impact of her novels from that of Hardy's.

Even when the individual himself is incapable of formulating this subjective experience, the novelist is able to exploit methods more readily available to him than to the dramatist who works within the terms of realism. George Eliot and Hardy in fact acknowledge the problems inarticulacy creates in realistic tragedy in order to exploit them. For the aesthetic problem derives from human problems which are part of the tragedy. Either lack of education or the modern habit of reticence prevents the open expression of feelings. As George Eliot puts it, 'we wrestle with the old sorrows, but more decorously' (*Felix Holt*, II, p. 212).

> Ah! That's the very feeling I've feeled over and over again, hostler, but not in such gifted language! 'Tis a thought I've had in me for years, and never could lick it into shape! O-ho-ho-ho! Splendid! Say it again, hostler, say it again! To hear my own poor notion that had no name brought into form like that.   (*The Hand of Ethelberta*, 1912, pp. 5–6.)

This is Hardy's formulation of the problem in comic terms, but he shows it to be far more often a source of tragedy. For his novels are concerned with the mass of people who are unable to articulate their own deepest thoughts and feelings and long for a spokesman. Denied the traditional rhetoric of the tragic hero, the individual is unable to communicate, burdened with a terrible isolation. When, on their wedding night, Tess tells Angel Clare of her seduction – in response to his own confessions – she loses him because she is unable, then or later, to follow her simple declaration with the 'glib and oily art' of persuasion and justification. But this lack of eloquence does not signify lack of feeling. There is something problematic in the relationship between language and experience, something not solved merely by education. Tess's School Standard English is no more adequate a vehicle for her feelings than her native dialect. On returning to his well-educated family, Angel finds his brothers particularly talkative, but notices their increasing mental limitations; they, in turn, notice his new quietness and that, instead, his face and eyes, like Tess's, have grown eloquent. Inarticulateness often suggests an awareness that language is inadequate to convey the profoundest experiences. Even the usually fluent character can find language useless to him, debased as it is by glib social usage. The 'second silent conversation' (*Jude the Obscure*, p. 244) Sue and Jude hold is a far more expressive means of communication.

George Eliot also recognises that the tragic experience renders the victim less, rather than more, articulate. But, in contrast with

Hardy's characters, as well as with the highly conscious Jamesian hero, this inarticulateness often seems pathetic instead of tragic, because the victim is unaware that the problem exists. A character like Hetty Sorrel is too absorbed in her own situation to be aware of the need for articulating it. On trial for the murder of her illegitimate child, her silence in the dock is pathetic, because she does not realise that she is letting slip by the opportunity to save herself. In order to give the experience of such a character a wider significance, George Eliot herself steps in and comments. Her intervention is often considered to be obtrusive and undramatic, but it creates a prophetic tone which confirms the deterministic vision, ironically underlining the individual's ignorance. It is her characteristic method of revealing what she calls 'that roar which lies on the other side of silence' (*Middlemarch*, I, pp. 297–8). Both she and Hardy try to articulate and universalise the individual's experience without putting false rhetoric into his mouth.

Henry James similarly exploits the problems his choice of subject raises. He sees the life of the upper classes in the late nineteenth century as being based on an ideal of decorum. If he is to reflect their life-style dramatically, as well as descriptively, the novelist requires the same decorum in his style. James also uses decorum as a theme, as a factor in the tragedy. For him, too, the aesthetic problem reflects a human one – the lack of outlet in word or deed for the individual's feelings and needs. The 'international' novels, in particular, highlight the limitations that the Old World's attention to form imposes on the American's frankness and thirst for freedom. The outspoken passion of Caspar Goodwood, Isabel Archer's American suitor, provides a stark contrast to the quiet understatement of his English counterpart, Lord Warburton. And Isabel's own freedom to speak with total frankness is as curtailed by her marriage to Osmond, the lover of the antique world, as is her freedom to act. The publicity in which such people live, their constant exposure to society even within their own drawing-rooms, increases the need to contain private grief. One of the characteristics of James's tragic novels is the tension between the private confusion and desperation, and the surface smoothness which results from the adherence to the idea of decorum. Suffering is increased because unexpressed:

> the grief that does not speak
> whispers the o'er-fraught heart and bids it break.

But this respect for decorum may be a form of protection. The value of keeping up appearances is evident in *The Wings of the Dove*. In Milly Theale's fatal illness, the reticence which prevents complete intimacy with other people is a guard as much against the doom-laden reality as against the prying interest of sym-pathisers. James implies that by refusing to acknowledge un-pleasant facts, the individual may minimise their impact, if not affect their existence. In *The Spoils of Poynton* Fleda Vetch sees her refusal to acknowledge her love for her benefactress's son, Owen Gereth, as her greatest protection from an illicit involvement with him: 'it only wanted words to be a committed act. . .her one thought was not to hear, to keep the act uncommitted' (p. 87). For James, speech marks the step from intention into action. The quietness which is characteristic of James's concept of tragedy as a private, internal matter is, therefore, reinforced by his thematic and formal use of decorum. Milly Theale never acts in any way which would broadcast to the world her illness or her grief over her betrayal by her friend, Kate, and Densher, the man she has grown to love. She simply turns her face to the wall. Even Roderick Hudson, the most vocal of men in his lifetime, finally takes his guilt and sorrow away into the mountains, to die there. In *Washington Square*, the heroine's Aunt Penniman assures the fortune-hunter Maurice Townsend that, whatever he does to her niece, 'the girl would be very quiet – she wouldn't make a noise' (p. 183).

And yet the very existence of such unspoken and unnoticed tragedies has terrifying implications for the nature of society. The narrator of *The Sacred Fount* (1901) observes May Server, whose beauty and youth are fading beneath the vampire-like onslaught of love, and is horrified by the 'beauty and terror of conditions so highly organised that under their rule her small lonely fight with disintegration could go on without the betrayal of a gasp or a shriek, and with no worse tell-tale contortion of lip or brow than the vibration. . .of that constantly renewed flower of amenity' (p. 132). Society is organised in such a way that everyone's attention is directed to the surfaces of life. Very few wish to look more closely. If the existence of violence and evil are once admitted, it will rupture the harmonious structure of civilised society. The forms no longer correspond to the content of life. James's hope is for an adjustment in society which will enable it to cope with evil more directly, as ideally it can, rather than relying on the act of faith involved in acting as if evil does not exist.

In the more formal sense, decorum is evident in James's neo-classical style of presentation. He usually avoids 'scenes' in the sense of emotional outbursts and moments of crisis. These are reported rather than enacted. The reader does not see Christina Light's final submission to her powerful mother, Owen Gereth's return to his strong-willed fiancée, Mona Brigstock, or Lord Mark's revelation of Kate and Densher's engagement to Milly. The physical manifestations of suffering and death are likewise omitted, as in classical tragedy. Milly's apparent lack of physical symptoms is typical of this reticence, which could be symbolised by Roderick Hudson's dead body – when it is found, the rain has washed away all the blood. The harsher side of life is concealed from the world at large, although it consumes the minds of those involved. Most of the time social small-talk fills the air, to the exclusion of those things filling the mind. As Ford Madox Ford commented,

that is how we really talk about the musical glasses whilst our lives crumble to pieces around us. . .the mind passes, as it does in real life, perpetually backwards and forwards between the apparent aspect of things and the essentials of life. . .That, you know, is what life really is – a series of such meaningless episodes beneath the shadow of doom – or of impending bliss.

(*Henry James, A Critical Study*, 1913, pp. 153–4.)

How then does James make the reader aware of the 'essentials of life'? The ideal of decorum combines with the demands of realism to prevent him from conveying this hidden layer of experience directly through the mouths of his characters. Disliking the first person narrative, what he calls 'the terrible *fluidity* of self-revelation',[5] he is denied that useful form of special pleading, of full, free, verbal expression. For a complete and consistent commentary on the situation James uses his '*ficelles*' – he gives us events as these observers perceive them. He gives us the character's vision as it takes shape, rather than after it has been tidied up and rationalised. Unlike George Eliot, James does not always filter the character's thoughts through his own intelligence, but presents them directly, as George Eliot herself does so successfully with Hetty's account of her child's birth and death. But because Hetty is such a limited, egotistic character, George Eliot finally intervenes to show the wider significance of her experience. James's technique depends, as I suggested in the previous chapter, on the use of highly aware central characters, able, like the author, to draw conclusions and make comparisons.

But there is a danger that these characters may seem too exceptionally gifted to be typical, as James himself readily admitted. It may, therefore, be necessary for this fine understanding to be at times false or confused, in the interests of human fallibility. As the reader sees the character in the process of forming his judgements, it is almost inevitable that – from ignorance of facts or of future developments – mistakes will be made. But it is less important for the vision to be always accurate, than for it to be always personal, for the reader to share the exclusive, individual experience, that has already been discussed in relation to Hardy and George Eliot. But just as the four main groups of characters in *Middlemarch* provide shifting perspectives, so James often provides changing viewpoints through his scenic method. Catherine Sloper's situation is tragic in the completeness with which it fills her life and in the utter emptiness it leaves behind. But when James registers Dr Sloper's vision, he introduces a strong element of irony, which the doctor uses to distance himself from the child, to enable him to relish the comedy in her predicament. Mrs Penniman sees the situation as romance, and again the element of irony appears in the gap between romance and reality. The multiplicity of aspects does not invalidate the individual's viewpoint – its truth lies in its sincerity – but demonstrates its partiality, stressing the inaccessibility of one soul to another. But in those novels in which James comes closest to the effects of tragedy, the tragic hero's exclusive viewpoint is emphasised because the other viewpoints converge on his – as all are centred on Isabel Archer and Milly Theale.

James's novels, therefore, are realistic only to the degree which is compatible with the ideal of restraint. The realism lies in the detailed presentation of the social setting, the fidelity with which its manners and *mores* are depicted. There is none of that realism of content so often associated with the late nineteenth-century novel – that is, the exposure of harsh and sordid physical realities. His tragedies are concerned with the common experience, but not the commonplace. Decorum holds in check any tendency to violence or excess which might result from attempting to portray the unexplored areas of human life. For James believes that violence of expression might produce many splendid effects, but destroys the fine shades and gradations which belong to truth.

(ii) REALISM AND SYMBOLISM

There is a very clear relationship between fact and fiction in the work of George Eliot and Thomas Hardy. Several passages from Hardy's article on 'The Dorsetshire Labourer' appear with very little alteration in *Tess of the D'Urbervilles*.[6] Hardy claims of the portrait he paints of rural life that 'at the dates represented in the various narrations things were like that in Wessex: the inhabitants lived in certain ways, engaged in certain occupations, kept alive certain customs, just as they are shown doing in these pages'.[7] The same kind of relationship exists between the comments George Eliot makes on working-class life in her review, 'The Natural History of German Life'[8] and her novels. The importance of factual detail to her is also evident in the extensive research she undertook for many of her novels – for the legal element in *Felix Holt*, for instance. But this wealth of sociological detail does not restrict the relevance of these novels to the life they portray. The representation of prosaic reality is for both writers the means of proceeding to the universal truths. As George Eliot observes, 'the language of all peoples soon attains to the expressions, ALL, UNIVERSAL, NECESSARY, but these expressions have their origins purely in the observations of the senses'.[9]

The scientific principles underlying each novelist's vision of life provide a rational counterpart to the Fates of Greek tragedy. Current ideas of heredity, evolution and environment act as contemporary and familiar symbols. This is particularly true of heredity, which Oscar Wilde called 'Nemesis without her mask. It is the last of the Fates and the most terrible.'[10] For Hardy it is a rendering of the Greek principle of collective or inherited guilt. Over the D'Urberville and Fawley families hovers a curse like that of the House of Atreus. George Eliot, as we have seen, uses heredity in a similar manner in *Felix Holt*, but for her Nemesis is embodied generally in the law of consequence. Guilt does not attack from outside, in the form of catastrophe, but manifests itself in the individual's conscience. Her Furies of Vengeance usually reside within the human breast. Maggie Tulliver tries to explain this to Stephen Guest, her cousin's fiancé, when he is trying to persuade her to run away with him. The memory of, and pity for, the sufferings she had caused those dearest to her would haunt her for the rest of her life, punishing her for seizing her chance of happiness at the expense of loyalty and duty.

In the work of both novelists there is a kind of dual notation, similar to that which is found in Hardy's epic drama, *The Dynasts* (1903–8). There the characters believe themselves to be listening to their consciences, while the reader sees them listening to the Spirits. There is both a rational, human interpretation, and a transcendental one which explains by reference to a non-human system. In literature that tries to relate the human to the non-human, there is room for the dual determination of classical tragedy. There is always an element that cannot be accounted for in purely rational terms: psychology itself summarises its findings in terms of a body of myths, as such terms as 'Oedipus complex' imply. The natural world of these novels is experienced both as a physical, and as a supernatural, influence. Its changes reflect forces that impinge on the individual's life at all levels. When Dinah Morris, the Methodist, after comforting Lisbeth Bede for the loss of her husband, returns from Loamshire to Snowfield in Stonyshire, the landscape changes and life gets harder not only physically, but morally. The changing seasons in Hardy's novels express the omnipotent rhythm of flux and reflux.

But although both novelists use Nature as part of the symbolic structure of their vision, they use it very differently. Hardy uses the natural image, such as is found in George Eliot's novels, less than the symbolic natural setting. George Eliot emphasises a character's place within the natural structure of the universe, suggesting his relationship with other men; Hardy isolates him in opposition to the natural world. George Eliot is less concerned with making him exceptional, with aggrandising the individual, than with suggesting that even the most ordinary man has an important place and function in the whole. Analogy is essential to her desire to 'only connect'. Where she makes particular connections, Hardy relies on the unspecified, but often archetypal associations conjured up by symbols. The microcosmic world of Middlemarch, with its politics and religious disputes, is connected with the progress of nineteenth-century England; Wessex is isolated from the rest of the world and, in the primitive barrenness of the heathland which dominates it, suggests the human arena itself. The urban world leaves less room for the supernatural to operate and raise the tale to the level of myth. The preponderance of scientific images in George Eliot's work typifies her precise, analytical use of metaphor. Her imagery works inwards, explaining itself in relation to other images, to clarify the philosophical complexity of her fictional world in a way that may help the reader to understand the complexity of his own. Her imagery has an explanatory function, because she believes understanding precedes sympathy. Hardy, however, believes that the reader cannot fully understand his characters unless he can share their feelings. He relies heavily on the emotive quality of symbolism, working outwards from the particular emotional quality of the experience to the more philosophical, more universal viewpoint.

For it is above all through symbolism that Hardy conveys and universalises the experience of the inarticulate. His realism gives ample expression to the facts of Tess's situation, but this is not enough.

> The exact truth as to material fact ceases to be of importance in art – it is a student's style – the style of a period when the mind is serene and unawakened to the tragical mysteries of life; when it does not bring anything to the object that coalesces with and translates the qualities that are already there – half hidden, it may be – and the two united are depicted as the all.
> (*Early Life*, p. 243.)

Hardy realises that to create tragedy out of commonplace private experience requires a careful adjustment between 'things unusual' and 'things eternal and universal'.[11] In the natural world of Wessex, Hardy finds an element of the universal which interacts both physically and psychologically with the unusual lives of its inhabitants. The effect this background has on the individual gives his symbols their psychological validity. When Michael Henchard goes to the ancient Roman Ring outside Casterbridge, to meet his former mistress, Lucetta, his attitude to her is affected by his memory of meeting the wife he had so badly wronged in that same place. The Ring, therefore, becomes a symbol of the cyclical repetitions of the past.

Hardy's use of symbolism is an example of what Henry James sees as a new aspect of contemporary art. It is a more analytic consideration of the appearance of things. It is known by its tendency to resolve its discoveries into pictorial form. It sees the connection between feelings and external conditions, and it expresses such relations as they have not been expressed hitherto. It deserves to win victories, because it has opened its eyes well to the fact that the magic of the arts of representation lies in their appeal to the associations awakened by things.

('Alphonse Daudet', *Century Illustrated Monthly Magazine*, 26, 1883, pp. 500–1.)

In his tendency to seek and find symbols, the Jamesian hero makes this connection between conditions and feelings. Often seeing themselves in literary terms, or as acting out roles, these characters interpret appearances in the light of their role. The symbol of the dove is offered to Milly Theale by an observer, as an interpretation of her character and way of life. It provides Milly with a role which she eagerly accepts. It suggests to her a psychological type, a manner of coping with her fate, and suggests to others how to cope with Milly. The very self-consciousness with which James's characters are involved in finding symbols in their lives highlights both the reality and its transmutation into universal terms. Before leaving America for Europe, Roderick Hudson smashes a bust of Mr Striker, the lawyer who was to have been his employer. The action is meant to express Roderick's exuberant anticipation of the future, and his delight at abandoning the legal profession and his dull past. But for Mary Garland the act indicates a dangerous change in his character; she suspects a purpose that is expressed so violently. For the reader, the action symbolises the unthinking destructiveness inherent in the egoist's ambition and idealism. The divergence between the meaning the protagonist puts into a symbolic action and that extracted from it reveals the unconscious as well as conscious workings of the mind.

James's symbolism is, therefore, integrated into the realistic content of the novel by the exceptional awareness of the 'free spirits'. What appears to be small talk frequently carries far deeper meanings because of its allusiveness. Between two highly aware individuals, the unspoken is not necessarily unshared. Either by means of indirect reference to the shared experience, or by the use of symbols, James's characters arrive at the centre of the issue, even if they do not openly acknowledge it. The symbols used frequently contain the violence and terror never otherwise expressed. These verbal images are brought to a climax and given dramatic expression in the rare – but for that reason, all the more effective – acts of violence which occur in the novels. Characters act as well as speak in symbols. The violence done to objects frequently carries the implication of violence to persons. Kate Croy's burning of Milly's last letter to Densher is such a gesture. Through these symbols the violent undercurrents come to the surface, and the effect is almost as shattering as the feared reality.

And it is through this symbolism that James establishes the validity of his heroes and heroines as human types. Their personal suffering is given heightened importance because it affects individuals who belong to an intellectual and social élite. This élite has, in turn, the same kind of universal validity as Shakespeare's kings and the Greek heroes: they represent the ideals of their society, ideals of fineness and high intelligence, even if society does not always recognise them as such. James is aware that it is not enough for these exceptional characters to be interesting in themselves, for 'the fictive hero successfully appeals to us only as an eminent instance, as eminent as we like, of our own conscious kind'.[12]

(iii) social tragedy: a contradiction in terms?

The traditional bias of the novel towards realism and the particular has been seen, in this chapter, continually to create problems for the novelist seeking to convey the universal truths of tragedy. The Victorian novel, furthermore, frequently portrays a very specific social and historical situation, its institutions, its *mores* and its manners. Many critics doubt whether true tragedy can arise from a social condition, because it must be related to whatever is unchanging and ubiquitous. If the causes of disaster lie in a particular situation, then could not that disaster be averted

simply by changing the situation, so that it is not, in fact, tragic –
that is, inevitable and universal? D.H. Lawrence's criticism of
Hardy represents such a position. He insists that Fate, or Nature,
should instigate tragedy and punish the tragic hero; society, the
substitute which writers like Hardy provide, is totally inadequate.
But is Lawrence correct in his analysis, in his assessment of 'the
weakness of modern tragedy, where transgression against the
social code is made to bring destruction, as though the social code
worked our irrevocable fate'?[18]

Novels in which social determination plays so large a part are
clearly vulnerable to such criticism. If social determinism accounts
for the whole complex of cause and effect, then it would seem
that the ensuing tragedy lies in the nature of society, and is not,
therefore, inevitable and universal, but relevant merely to a
particular time and place. The subject of working-class tragedy
seems even more questionable. The conditions out of which
suffering arises are temporal and – in the long term – temporary.
The suffering also relates to a particular sector of society, rather
than, at first glance, to 'man'. And yet the novelists under discussion relate their sectional, social interests to wider issues in a
way that disproves this kind of tragic theory.

Even George Eliot's earliest novels are never exclusively concerned with one particular class. Where she concentrates on working-class life, she emphasises not the poverty which divides them
from other people, but the joys and sorrows common to all. In
bringing out the capacity for tragic experience in ordinary work-
ing-men, she is suggesting not that working-class life is essentially
tragic, but that all life is potentially so. She is not concerned with
isolating their tragedy, but with relating it to the rest of society.
George Eliot does not attempt to express the experience of belonging to an underprivileged mass. Although her conception of the
Jews in *Daniel Deronda* is potentially tragic, the sense of tragedy
is not impressed upon the reader because the emphasis is on
Daniel, who finds happiness in his race just as Adam finds it in
his station. Alternatively, a man like Felix Holt can find happiness

by leaving his class, so that the problems of the working-class never become more than a historical background. None of her characters finds his class alone a bar to happiness. The working-class, like the Jewish race, is chosen as a subject not merely for its intrinsic interest, but to stretch the contemporary middle-class reader's sympathy to the limits, against all preconceived ideas and natural inclinations, as a necessary progression to universal sympathy.

Hardy, however, does bring the tragedy of the underprivileged to the fore. Class distinctions stand in the way of Jude's ambitions as surely as they encourage Tess's subjection to Alec. Poverty completes their destruction. Its miserable consequences are evident not only in the lives of the central characters, but in the lives of those who occupy the background, the many those few represent. Such problems are to some degree ephemeral: conditions have improved. But Hardy shows that these specific conditions arise from man's tragically persistent inhumanity to man. Hardy's social concerns are apparent everywhere. He shows the misery caused by changing economic and social pressures, arising out of humanity's indifference to itself. But he sees beyond this the tragic fact of death, and the utter loneliness it imposes on each individual. This inevitable and irremediable fact perhaps causes humanity's indifference, but it makes it all the more poignant.

If neither George Eliot nor Hardy is concerned exclusively with one group, then the same kind of argument can be used in relation to James's concentration on a social élite, and in relation to the emphasis he gives to nationality, and the very specific American–European confrontation. His critique of both the Old and New Worlds implies an alternative, a society which would not give rise to such tragic situations and which could cope more adequately with the evils which occur. But what is important is the expectation that evil will continue to occur. Each society creates its own particular forms of suffering, but James suggests that tragedy derives from the less tangible imperfections of human nature. It derives, as it does in George Eliot's novels, from universal moral conflicts which turn human relationships into exploitation and alienation. It arises out of the conflict between the individual and the mass which assumes the right to overrule all considerations of individuality. It is for his understanding of this universal tragedy that Ezra Pound defends James against accusations of triviality and an excessive concern with superficial manners.

What I have not heard is any word of the major James, of the hater of tyranny; book after early book against oppression, against all the sordid petty personal crushing oppression, the domination of modern life, not worked out in the diagrams of Greek tragedy, not labelled 'epos' or 'Aeschylus'... What he fights is 'influence', the impinging of family pressure, the impinging of one personality on another.

('Brief Note', *Little Review*, 5, 1918, p. 7.)

If Pound refers here to 'modern life', it is not as a limiting factor, any more than is the label 'Greek', but merely in order to relate James's theme to its immediate subject. Tragedy exists in its own atemporal timescale as much as in the era of its setting.

But critics still sometimes suggest that, even if society is used only as the tragic machinery, rather than the ultimate cause, then the result will be poetically weak. Karl Jaspers puts it this way: 'The very transparency of these alternatives exhausts the problem. Where there is no sense of the infinite vastness of what is beyond our grasp, all we finally succeed in conveying is misery – not tragedy.'[14] In his use of the natural setting, Hardy provides this sense of vastness in an immediately impressive physical form. In contrast, the detailed social settings of George Eliot's and James's novels makes the infinite and elemental less obvious and forceful, although present on a philosophical, abstract level. Hardy's use of Nature, moreover, compensates for any limitations his characters may have as individuals. Unelevated as they are, they assume the significance and stature of tragic heroes: 'isolation on a heath renders vulgarity well-nigh impossible'.[15] They are associated more with the primitive landscapes of Wessex than with any particular village. These scenes symbolise the universe: offering little shelter from the elements, they remind us of the principle of

change, of death and decay, but also of the principle of rebirth
and continuity. Exposed to them, each character becomes mere
man, with all the tragedy, pathos and grandeur that implies. The
exception is Jude, who is mainly seen in the city, but here Hardy is
trying to create something significantly different, as I hope to
demonstrate.

Neither George Eliot's nor James's vision of 'what is beyond
our grasp' – in their case the complex web of society – has any
single physical manifestation, so that their vision tends to lack the
emotive power which the symbol of Wessex generates. And, as
far as the 'background' of their novels is concerned, it may be
relevant to quote the comments of G.K. Chesterton.

Man is merely man only when he is seen against the sky. If he is seen
against landscape, he is only a man of that land. If he is seen against any
house, he is only a householder. Only where death and eternity are present
can human beings fully feel their fellowship. Once the divine darkness against
which we stand is really dismissed from the mind (as it was very nearly dismissed in Victorian time) the *differences* between human beings become
overpoweringly plain.

(The Victorian Age in Literature, p. 60.)

The characters of George Eliot and Henry James inhabit a
primarily social world, a world of buildings and institutions. The
differences between human beings are consequently much more
in evidence. But this awareness of differences is paradoxically the
universal truth both novelists convey. Pound describes it – in connection with James – as a recognition of 'the right of differences
to exist, of interest in finding things different' ('Brief Note', p. 9).
They want a universal tolerance which will take into account and
welcome the sense of difference because it makes a valuable contribution to their fellowship.

It may be said, in fact, that all tragedy is related to a social
situation or crisis, but transcends it. As George Eliot writes of the
Antigone:

we no longer believe that to neglect funeral rites is to violate the claims of
the infernal deities. But these beliefs are the accidents and not the substance
of the poet's conception. The turning-point of the tragedy is not. . .'rever-

ence for the dead, etc.'. . .but the *conflict* between these and obedience to the State. Here lies the dramatic collision. . .an antagonism between valid claims. ('The *Antigone* and its Moral', *Leader*, 29 March, 1856, p. 306.)

But it would be a great mistake to discount the social, contemporary elements in the tragedies these novelists portray. For one of the advantages the novel possesses over drama as a medium for tragedy is the depth and detail with which it can depict the seemingly trivial forms in which the elements of tragedy encroach upon and destroy the individual's happiness. These novelists promote our awareness of the different kinds of suffering which each era, each historical change, may bring about. Each tries to ensure that the reader is not blinded to the tragedy around him by a stereotyped image of tragedy, that he recognises the new forms of barbarity which civilisation may give rise to. For, although it may be argued that the possibility of change lessens the possibility of tragedy, the fate of the individual trapped in his own era remains tragic. If the character convinces us and wins our sympathy on his own terms, his fate must overshadow any optimistic faith in social change. The greater the faith, the greater the sense of waste in any particular instance. And the tragedy lies in the waste. For each of these novelists makes the same plea: 'I care for the people who live now and will not be living when the long-run comes.' (*Felix Holt*, II, p. 36.)

4

GEORGE ELIOT: PATHOS AND TRAGEDY

(i) PATHETIC TRAGEDY

George Eliot's fidelity to life continually and deliberately under-
mines the movement of her novels towards tragedy. The heroes
of her domestic tragedies – whom she so often describes as 'poor'
– lack the aesthetic appropriateness, awareness and articulacy
which belong to the traditional tragic hero. They appeal to our
sympathy because of their weaknesses, rather than their strengths.
And yet she succeeds in making these characters the focus for the
tragic response, because her own consciousness of tragedy en-
closes them, fusing together the elements of pathos and tragedy.
She conveys, therefore, a kind of tragedy, the only kind – she
implies – that will reflect the nature of her society.

The traditional tragic hero's appropriateness lies largely in his
dignity, and his willingness to stake everything on his struggle.
These qualities arouse the spectator's awe and reverence, responses
that may be absent from real life, where pity has become increasingly more common than reverence. But in realistic tragedy, these
qualities are even more important, for they, rather than predestined status, are what ensure the individual's heroic stature.
Arthur Miller in his essay on 'Tragedy and the Common Man',
considers total commitment is one of the essential characteristics
that make the ordinary man an adequate subject for tragedy.[1]
For Miller, the hero's guilt lies in the completeness of his defiance
and demands as extreme a punishment. The punishment may be
a logical consequence of a particular crime, as Tess Durbeyfield's
execution follows on her murder of Alec D'Urberville. But what

is really being punished is the heroine's or hero's refusal to come
to terms with his situation, his declaration – explicit or implicit –
that even life itself is not worth a compromise. In contrast, George
Eliot's characters share the desire to save all that they can of their
wrecked lives. She shows how men cling to life with pathetic
despair, even when it has been robbed of all its promise. Even
when she has lost her lover, and killed her own child, Hetty Sorrel's awareness of her own warm, live flesh makes suicide impossible to her, and transportation infinitely preferable to the gallows.
Her choice may be the natural, human one, but it is one we cannot imagine an Antigone or a Cordelia making. Even the elderly
Edward Casaubon of *Middlemarch*, facing the futility of his
life's work and the disappointment that his marriage to young
Dorothea Brooke has failed to awaken his heart and bring him
happiness, recoils from the so-called escape that death offers.

A. Miller's view of tragedy

> When the commonplace 'We must all die' transforms itself suddenly into
> the acute consciousness 'I must die – and soon', then death grapples us,
> and his fingers are cruel;...And Mr Casaubon's immediate desire was not
> for divine communion and light divested of earthly conditions; his passion-
> ate longings, poor man, clung low and mist-like in very shady places.
>
> (*Middlemarch*, II, p. 230.)

In the essay already mentioned, Arthur Miller stipulates one other
condition:

and isn't there w/ Hardy

> The possibility of victory must be there in tragedy. Where pathos rules, a
> character has fought a battle he could not possibly have won. Pathos is
> truly the mode for the pessimist. But tragedy requires a nicer balance
> between what is possible and what is not. (p. 3)

Hardy has often been called a pessimist, but the 'balance' is pre-
served in his novels by his use of Chance, which continually implies how close the individual comes to success. George Eliot is
certainly concerned to stress the distinction between the possible
and the impossible. But the possibility of victory for her pathetic
characters is undermined by their lack of awareness of either their
own situation, or of anyone else's. They do not simply fail to
estimate the odds correctly, taking on more than they can cope

with, but they fail to recognise that battle has commenced, that struggle is a necessary and inevitable aspect of life. The tragedy for characters as different as Casaubon and Hetty Sorrel is that they have little sense of either the depths or heights of human life, its hazards or its possibilities.

Hetty provides, of course, the outstanding example of pathetic tragedy in George Eliot's work. As Henry James notes, the novelist avoids 'the easy error of representing her as in any degree made serious by suffering'.[2] Hetty's last meeting with Dinah Morris, the Methodist, in the prison cell, enables her to confess and once more make human contact, but she is denied the strength and wisdom which traditionally accompany tragic suffering. Without Dinah, she would collapse, literally and metaphorically. There is no triumph in her suffering, for she does not sufficiently understand its meaning to rise above it, either in heroic defiance or in conscious self-sacrifice as recognition of her common humanity. The reader can only feel pity for her incapacitating incomprehension, rather than sympathy for a suffering equal.

But while Hetty herself is pathetic, her situation taken as a whole is not. She is incapable of the tragic response, of expressing or even realising the significance of her predicament. Her experience is too big for her, just as her outer beauty is disproportionate to the shallow nature it conceals; hers is one of those faces 'which nature charges with a meaning and pathos not belonging to the single human soul that flutters beneath them, but speaking the joys and sorrows of foregone generations' (*Adam Bede*, 1, p. 430). Like the child or kitten with which she is so often compared, Hetty is not fully developed as a human being. The tragedy of man's destiny is too vast and generalised a concept to be within her grasp. And yet this very unawareness is itself tragic. The contrast between the pathetic and tragic ideal itself evokes the pity and the terror of the tragic response. Hetty's passionate clinging to life is a disturbing contrast to the traditional hero's espousal of death. She reminds us of the gulf between what we might be and what we are. She also reminds us of the even more terrible gulf

[margin handwritten note: tragedy without a hero?]

between even the most reduced form of life, and death, the unknown quantity that makes cowards of us all. Casaubon's lack of
awareness is unrelated to any lack of sophistication, but his situation elicits a similar response. Just as Hetty's exceptional experience is too much for her, so the most common experiences are too
much for him. His agony is 'to be present at this great spectacle
of life and never to be liberated from a small, hungry, shivering
self' (*Middlemarch*, II, p. 12).

This shrouding of the pathetic individual in the author's sense *author controls*
of awe at the human condition can be called pathetic tragedy. *our Response*
Paradoxically, the moment that the reader feels the absence and
impossibility of traditional tragedy is the moment that he comes
closest to George Eliot's tragic sense. Arising naturally from her
emphasis on the passivity of the domestic world, and the lives of
the women who inhabit it, pathos consistently qualifies her tragic
fiction.

(ii) PATHOS AND THE WOMAN'S TRAGEDY

Female characters occupy a central position in the work of many
novelists of the period, male and female. Women novelists as
varied as the Brontës, George Eliot, Mrs Gaskell and Mrs Oliphant could be said to be simply writing about what they knew
best. But Hardy's women are also generally agreed to be more
successful than his men, and the number of heroines, as opposed
to heroes, in the work of Henry James is striking. Even in novels
with titles like *Daniel Deronda*, *Felix Holt* and *Roderick Hudson*,
the predicament of the main female character threatens to overshadow the career of the hero. And this is only partly the result
of the emphasis on the domestic life. Even the most famous epic
novel of the period – Thackeray's *Vanity Fair* – might be considered, in its creator's phrase, 'a novel without a hero' if only
because the dominant figure of Becky Sharp overshadows her
male counterparts. The growing interest in feminist issues, implicit in Charlotte Brontë's studies of governesses and teachers and

explicit in *Jude the Obscure* and *The Bostonians*, may be a factor, but James for one stated that he was bored by the 'woman question'. Even George Eliot eliminates most of her references to the contemporary situation of women from the final draft of the 'Finale' to *Middlemarch*. What, then, is the reason for the focus on women? In the work of the three novelists under discussion, woman has a representative value which goes beyond any specific social statement.

Womanhood is primarily significant in George Eliot's novels because it is the most immediate and overwhelming of deterministic factors. Biologically, the 'weaker sex' is made dependent on men by the burden of childbearing. And socially, the influence of women on men is in the long run only the power to choose their own 'lord and master'. In Caleb Garth, the honest land agent of Middlemarch, George Eliot probably recreated her memories of her own father. He warns his daughter, Mary, that a woman, 'let her be as good as she may, has got to put up with the life her husband makes for her' (1, 393). Unable to determine her own fate, a woman is liable to suffer from events which she has played no part in bringing about. Her fate is pathetic, for she is morally guiltless, but also tragic, for she is nevertheless implicated in the family's guilt.

These problems are exacerbated by the prevailing social climate. Each sex receives a different kind of upbringing, reflecting for George Eliot society's tendency to treat an individual as a member of a group or class, paying no attention to his particular need or abilities. The childhood of Tom and Maggie Tulliver illustrates this at length. Maggie's obvious aptitude for learning is totally neglected, while great care is lavished on providing the best education for Tom, despite his unfitness for it. For the general view is that 'a woman's no business wi' being so clever' (*The Mill on the Floss*, 1, p. 20). If Maggie's cleverness leads to trouble, fulfilling Mr Tulliver's fears, it is only because it is given no proper nourishment or outlet. It turns into tormenting introspection and an overwhelming hunger for beauty and enlightenment.

Cleverness becomes a blow [margin note]

If women are denied a proper education, it is because 'it doesn't signify what they think – they are not called upon to judge or to act' (*Felix Holt*, 1, p. 56). They are seen in purely domestic roles, ideally as wife and mother. Lydgate at first finds Dorothea too earnest, inconceivable as a wife because impossible to relax with. In spite of his unconventional views on the medical profession, he clings to the conventional view of marriage. Rosamund Vincy, he feels, will fulfil her role perfectly, for she is 'instructed to the true womanly limit' and has 'the innate submissiveness of the goose'.[3] But what Lydgate regards as Rosamund's essential femininity makes her totally inadequate as a partner: so engrossed is she in the female 'arts' that she is unable to share her husband's interests and problems, or to establish any realistic relationship with the world from which she has been so protected. Their marriage, like others, leads to a tragic clash between love and ambition. Lydgate is rapidly disillusioned. But he cannot claim that Rosamund has deceived him. He has deceived himself about the nature of marriage. If woman can create havoc in men's lives, this is as much the fault of men as of women.

And yet Dorothea's totally unconventional conception of marriage proves equally disastrous. For even she accepts some of the conventional distinctions between men and women, particularly the superior capacity of the male for learning and greatness. Rather than seeking partnership, she hopes to fulfil herself through her husband's ambition, attempting to live vicariously. Her vision of marriage as a father-daughter relationship suggests that it is her own development and instruction that she seeks, not a husband. Casaubon is as much a means to an end for Dorothea as Lydgate is for Rosamund. If marriage so often appears destructive, it is not in the nature of the union itself, as the strength-giving relationship of the Garths indicates. It is because society and individuals alike have false notions of it, forcing every individual into a stereotyped role regardless of fit.

Although this clash between essence and function exists for both husband and wife, it is more evident in women because of

the narrowness of their traditional role. Ambition is a male pre-
rogative. It can only be fulfilled by great sacrifices. Daniel
Deronda's mother sacrifices her own personal life – even her son –
in order to fulfil herself as an actress. She protests to her son:

Every woman is supposed to have the same set of motives, or else to be a
monster...I cared for the wide world, and all that I could represent in
it...You are not a woman. You may try – but you can never imagine
what it is to have a man's force of genius in you, and yet to suffer the
slavery of being a girl.   (*Daniel Deronda*, iii, pp. 130–1.)

And opportunities are not necessarily increased by wealth. In
spite of her independence of means, Dorothea suffers from 'the
stifling oppression of that gentlewoman's world where everything
was done for her and none asked for her aid' (*Middlemarch*, ii,
p. 3). Even Gwendolen Harleth gradually realises the emptiness
of existence for someone who has only been taught to be a charm-
ing young lady. Being denied a function, being expected to be
mere ornament, is appalling to those who, like Maggie, find plain
sewing with a purpose more to their liking than embroidery.

The passivity thus enforced upon women makes them outstanding examples of pathetic tragedy. Maggie's grief is continually
exacerbated by her helplessness to affect either the family fortunes
or her own. The true male 'would rather go and slay the Nemean
lion or perform any round of heroic labours than endure perpetual
appeals to his pity for evils over which he can make no conquest'.
A woman has no such means of venting her feelings: 'so it has
been since the days of Hecuba, and of Hector, Tamer of horses'.[4]
While men may fight, women must weep and wait. Gwendolen
always attempts to escape from thought in action, particularly on
horseback. She experiences real suffering as Grandcourt gradually
curtails her movement, finally marooning her in the enclosed
arena of his yacht. A woman's conflicts are internal and unseen.
George Eliot is rarely concerned with those more traditional
tragic heroines who, like Antigone, are active rebels.

Women are, therefore, a symbol not only of George Eliot's
characteristic vision of tragedy, but also of her idea of heroism.

They represent the essential quality of resignation and the values of the heart, safeguarding them against the values of the male world – the world of business, struggle and ambition. Woman is the guardian of tenderness and spontaneous warmth, suppressed in men by social convention: 'that ardour of hers which breaks through formulas too rigorously urged on men by daily practical needs, makes one of her most precious influences' (*Felix Holt*, II, p. 313). Moreover, a woman's love is essentially Christian, in that it is a love which is unconditional and merciful, as opposed to the love of the Old Testament God of justice, which must be earned. George Eliot offers this ideal love as an alternative to the patriarchal principle which plays so dominant a role in Victorian society, distinguishing, for instance, between the deserving and undeserving poor.

[handwritten margin note: ? Mrs. Poyser? Gwendolen? Dodson women?]

George Eliot would agree with Henry James's feminist heroine of *The Bostonians*, Verena Tarrant, that women's bitterest fate is 'to see so clearly and not to be able to do' (II, 56–7). But she feels that something can be achieved even in passivity, through this feminine strength of feeling. She explains her attitude in a letter to John Morley:

> as a fact of mere zoological evolution, woman seems to me to have the worse share of existence. But for that very reason I would the more contend that in the moral evolution we have 'an art which does mend nature'. It is the function of love in the largest sense, to mitigate the harshness of all fatalities. (*George Eliot Letters*, IV, p. 364.)

Men suffer as much as women from the neglect of those values so necessary to life. The subjection of women to a limited, conventional role is symbolic of the universal tragedy – the stifling of individual intuitions and emotions by organised social structures. If this subjection is accepted, civilisation must stagnate, but each protest against it, however ineffectual, contributes to the moral progress of mankind. It is because of their central position in her moral universe that George Eliot gives women and their domesticity so dominant a place in her novels. Discussing the American

Civil War in *Daniel Deronda*, she answers the question which this domestic focus might raise:

What in the midst of that mighty drama are girls and their blind visions? They are the Yea or Nay of that good for which men are enduring and fighting. In these delicate vessels is borne onward through the ages the treasure of human affections. (I, 182.)

(iii) 'THE MILL ON THE FLOSS'

In this novel George Eliot combines the basic elements of her vision of modern tragedy – the woman's situation, with its enforced passivity and pathos, and the stifling of the individual by artificial social roles – with more traditional concepts of tragedy. She abandons the happy-ending convention, proposing no answer to the riddle of life. The novel repeats the conflict that she sees in *Antigone* – 'an antagonism between valid claims'.[5] This conflict creates an insoluble tension which makes the compromise characteristic of George Eliot's novels impossible. The form of the novel is consequently moulded by the tragic vision. The pathetic is here transformed into unqualified tragedy. The novel therefore deserves special consideration.

The detailed portrait of childhood given in this novel emphasises the effect of heredity and environment. Mr Tulliver's business downfall further distorts his children's natural lines of development, thrusting adult sorrows and responsibilities upon them. In spite of their own innocence, Maggie and Tom become implicated in their father's tragedy and guilt when they are made to swear upon the family bible to continue the family feud with the Wakems, Mr Tulliver's business rivals. The endless cycle of revenge keeps turning, regardless of right or wrong, innocence or guilt: 'so deeply inherent is it in this life of ours that men have to suffer for each other's sins, so inevitably diffusive is human suffering, that even justice makes its victims, and we can conceive no retribution that does not spread beyond its mark in pulsations of unmerited pain'.[6] The revenge theme which dominates Greek

But is Maggie's "wise passiveness"?

and Jacobean tragedy here gives dramatic force to George Eliot's
law of consequences.

But while both children inherit their father's destiny, only
Maggie inherits those aspects of his character which make such
a destiny finally tragic. The 'pitiable, furious bull entangled in
the meshes of a net' (I, 395) is reincarnated in his daughter. But
Mr Tulliver's passionate impulsiveness becomes in Maggie an
impulse to love, rather than to violence and hate. There is nothing
in Tom to conflict with his father's desire for revenge. But
Maggie's family loyalty clashes with that affection for Philip
Wakem which is associated with her desire for fulfilment. To
break with her family would itself diminish her identity. But can
duty lie in that feudal hatred against which every fibre of her
heart cries out?

The internal conflict between these irreconcilable claims is intensified by externals. Maggie's intellectual starvation in the isolation of the mill is like a 'long suicide' (II, 97). It is because she
has been so deprived of the worlds of beauty, intellect and tenderness that her meeting with Philip and later Stephen Guest, her
cousin's fiancé, make so great an onslaught on her family loyalties.
George Eliot places less faith than usual in the strength of the
will:

the tragedy of our lives is not created entirely from within. 'Character',
says Novalis, in one of his questionable aphorisms – 'character is destiny'.
But not the whole of our destiny. (II, 210)

Moral judgement is here tempered by reference to special circumstances. But Maggie's moments of weakness are not glossed over.
For the individual should accept unhappiness for himself, rather
than seek happiness at the expense of others. Maggie and Stephen
Guest allow themselves small failures – small intimacies and in-
discretions – in their last few days together before Maggie's planned departure from St Ogg's. They rely on events to separate
them. When events instead bring them together, the habit of
yielding has been established. On returning to St Ogg's after

being adrift on the river with Stephen, Maggie finds 'the consequences of such a fall had come before the outward act was
completed' (II, 322). There is justice in it. If we accept her unfulfilled aspirations as heroic, then we are also bound to accept her
yielding – although incomplete – as tragic and punishable. Society
may be wrong, but the artistic logic is right.

George Eliot's description of Maggie as 'a character essentially
noble but liable to great error – error that is anguish to its own
nobleness',[7] suggests a heroine conceived in Aristotelian terms.
She bears that tragic guilt which takes the novel beyond the realm
of pathetic tragedy. For her error derives from her impulsiveness,
and the strength of her emotions: her weakness is simultaneously
her strength as a loving human being. The line between egoism
and altruism is at times very fine. Maggie initially sees renunciation as a dramatic role to give her a feeling of importance: 'that
is the path we all like when we set out on our abandonment of
egoism – the path of martyrdom and endurance, where the palm-
branches grow, rather than the steep highway of tolerance, just
allowance, and self-blame' (II, 39). Until her painful and genuine
renunciation of Stephen, Maggie is playing with a romantic
version of sacrifice. And yet her faults are more to be respected
than the righteousness of her brother. Maggie herself tells Tom,
'sometimes when I have done wrong, it has been because I have
feelings that you would be the better for, if you had them' (II,
125). And in spite of her criticism of Tom, she is free from
complacency: ' "I'd do just the same again." That was Tom's
usual mode of viewing his past actions; whereas Maggie was always wishing she had done something different' (I, 77). Maggie's
self-doubts are her spiritual salvation, enabling her to learn. Man
must lose his innocence to become fully human. It is characteristic
of the tragic hero that he is destroyed by the very qualities that are
admirable: even as a child, Maggie is punished more often than
Tom – not because she is naughtier, but because less calculating.
For in this novel, the survival of the fittest is not the survival of

[margin note:] good – & it is especially true that Maggie's virtues are not appreciated in a world domina- ted by Dodsonian oppressiveness

the best. The principle of sacrifice is less optimistically portrayed than elsewhere in George Eliot's work. The novel portrays
'the suffering, whether of martyr or victim, which belongs to
every historical advance of mankind' (II, 6). But George Eliot's
view of history as a progression is replaced by a view of history as
a repetitive cycle of upheaval and sacrifice, symbolised by the recurrent flooding. Maggie's suffering is a necessary part in the
evolutionary process, for she is almost the only inhabitant of St
Ogg's to be sensitive to the complexity of the past and present
around her. But this apparent necessity in no way represents an
ideal. The natural law is at odds with the moral law.

yes : Maggie's greater sensitivity

There is no way of dealing justly with all concerned. There can
be no solution, only an ending. Maggie effectually chooses death
rather than compromise. The flood warnings coincide with Dr
Kenn's suggestion that she should leave St Ogg's, but the prospect
of exile is like death to her. When the flood comes, Maggie's return to the mill shows her instinctive desire for a reconciliation
with her family and her past which will restore her wholeness,
even at the cost of life. She retraces the steps by which she departed
from her integrity by running away with Stephen. Again she
moves by impulse, but this time by the impulse to return to her
origins, not to escape them. This is 'the transition of death, without its agony' (II, 393) – the one moment when Maggie finds
fulfilment, when her whole being is intent upon a single purpose.
Death itself comes as a kind of joy, in Tom's arms. Throughout
the novel joy and sorrow, triumph and tragedy, are intermingled,
and its ending brings this theme to a climax. Death comes as a
kind of vindication. We are reminded of Maggie's childhood
comments on the picture of the witch being drowned: 'if she's
drowned – and killed, you know – she's innocent, and not a
witch, but only a poor silly old woman. But what good would it
do her then, you know, when she was drowned? Only, I suppose,
she'd go to heaven, and God would make it up to her' (I, 21). As
an adult, Maggie provides a different answer. Without hope of

benefiting herself, she insists that '*some* good will come by clinging to the right' (II, 334).

Because George Eliot here follows her tragic vision to its
logical conclusion, allowing it to dominate the novel thematically,
and through the structure of events, the novel has a stricter form
than is usual in George Eliot's work. *Silas Marner* shows structural similarities to *The Mill on the Floss*: it has the cyclical pattern which results from the emphasis on the past and on Nemesis,
but the novel's overall pattern is just rather than tragic because
the hero is so complete a victim. *Silas Marner* has the form of a
moral fable, rather than of a tragedy. George Eliot writes of the
earlier novel, 'my love of the childhood scenes made me linger
over them; so that I could not develop as fully as I wished the
concluding "Book" in which the tragedy occurs, and which I had
looked forward to with much attention and premeditation from
the beginning'.[8] That the flood was part of the initial plan is con-
firmed by the novelist's research in the British Museum. But it is
also evident from the novel itself. References to the floods of the
past and to possible recurrences, hints that Maggie will come to a
bad end, and Mrs Tulliver's fears of her children drowning, all
combine with the associated image-patterns to suggest what is in
store. The river is a symbol of Maggie's impulsiveness: we have
to wait for her destiny 'to reveal itself like the course of an un-
mapped river; we only know that the river is full and rapid, and
that for all rivers there is the same final home (II, 221). There
may be no causal connection between Maggie's infringement of
the social code and her death, but the imagery acts as a shorthand
for the destructiveness of impulse, suggesting that Maggie will be
destroyed in some such natural climax.

The return to the beginning also gives the novel the cyclical
structure typical of tragedy. The pattern is evident in the revenge
theme. Each step Maggie takes towards a better future brings her
face to face with the past, in the form of the family vendetta, or in
the form of her own conscience, constantly accusing her of dis-
loyalty. The cyclical pattern is evident, too, in the series of ironic

reversals resulting from attempts to direct the future and evade the inevitable, from Mrs Tulliver's appeal to Wakem to Lucy's attempt to reunite Philip and Maggie.

As the individual's life is set in this repetitive pattern, it becomes simply one of many, universalised so as to raise the private sorrow to the level of tragedy. And this universal quality is highlighted by those elements of isolation that are more common in Hardy's novels.[9] Maggie is one of

> The souls by nature pitched too high,
> By suffering plunged too low. (11, 265)

Both in her ambitions and in her grief she is set apart from the rest of society. The intensity of her passions, even in childhood, is enough 'to have made a tragedy, if tragedy were made by passion only' (1, 154). Maturity and her family's plight give these passions the essential seriousness and magnitude. The primitive, overwhelming attraction she feels for Stephen has an impersonal quality which isolates her from the other characters, including Stephen himself, who seek satisfaction within the normal conventions of society. Even before tragedy intrudes, the whole Tulliver family is detached from society. At the mill, they are associated with a natural order, rather than the civilised world of St Ogg's. In spite of the veneer of cultivation which Mrs Tulliver attempts to impose on their lives, Tom and Maggie absorb some of the primitive qualities of the earth and water to which they live so close.

In such a situation, the supernatural takes a powerful hold on the imagination, and the protagonists themselves seem caught up in the aura of myth and legend. St Ogg – whose motto is, 'it is enough that thy heart needs it' (1, 180) – seems an incongruous patron for the town whose patron he is, but he represents an ideal that periodically rises to the surface in individuals like Maggie. The saint does not manifest himself to save Maggie from the flood, but he appears with the Virgin in a dream which is decisive in reminding her of Lucy and Tom, and their needs. The legend that St Ogg will appear during a flood to give new hope and strength to those battling against the stream is, in symbolic terms, fulfilled. Aligned with such myths, the story of Maggie Tulliver becomes itself a symbol for all time: the accidents of time and place are finally irrelevant to the real tragedy.

(iv) EXCURSIONS INTO HEROIC TRAGEDY: 'THE SPANISH GYPSY', 'FELIX HOLT' AND 'DANIEL DERONDA'

A good tragic subject must represent a possible, sufficiently probable, not a common action; and to be really tragic, it must represent irreparable collision between the individual and the general. . .It is the individual with whom we sympathise, and the general of which we recognise the irresistible power.

In these notes on *The Spanish Gypsy* (1868), George Eliot describes the same 'collision' that is represented in her novels. But the idea that the tragic action should be uncommon is new. The tragedy of the everyday has given way to that of the exceptional. Her dramatic poem reverses the tragic situation in her novels: 'A young maiden, believing herself to be on the eve of the chief event of her life – marriage – about to share in the ordinary lot of womanhood, full of young hope, has suddenly announced to her that she is chosen to fulfil a great destiny, entailing a terribly different experience from that of ordinary womanhood'.[10] It is usually the experience of ordinary womanhood that thwarts the individual's fulfilment. George Eliot's dramatic poem represents a shift from pathetic to heroic tragedy, a shift which at first sight appears to carry over into *Felix Holt* and *Daniel Deronda*.

Heroic tragedy is the tragedy of individuals exceptional both in terms of inner qualities and in terms of their position in society. 'Born leaders', in both senses of the term, their actions are of great significance to their people. The close bond between the private and the public life which we find in the novels is even more evident here as we see Don Silva, the Spanish Commandant, trying to keep his private relationship with Fedalma, the gypsy, distinct from his public obligations. And while the leader must accept his role with that resignation which for George Eliot is a major constituent of heroism, he must fulfil his role with 'heroic Promethean effort'.[11] The nobly heroic, usually held suspect by the novelist, finds a valid place in fifteenth-century Spain.

But heroism is not valued merely for its achievements:

> The greatest gift the hero leaves his race
> Is to have been a hero. (i, 130)

As wanderers, with no god and therefore no divine law – no sense of why they exist or where they are going, the gypsies desperately need such a hero as they find in their chief, Zarca. His 'deeds of such divine beneficence' (i, 115) will establish an ideal that will unify the people. And the hero's consciousness of race, of the group, extends the significance of each moment in his life. It gives him that heightened awareness of 'the general' which characterises the tragic consciousness.

The racial issues involved in the individual's struggle give the subject a grander scale than is usual in George Eliot's work. The characters are here seen in relation to history, rather than in relation to nature, as in the early novels. Nature and evolutionary theory reduce each individual to the same level, as a minute speck in the process of evolution. History, in contrast, appears as a series of unique events, changing the shapes of maps and genealogies. Events such as occur in *The Spanish Gypsy* are apparently triggered off by exceptional individuals such as Prior Isidor, the Inquisitor. The portentousness of the occasion depicted in this dramatic poem combines with its remote setting to give that heightened sense of reality which is commoner in drama than the novel because of the greater foreshortening and stylisation required by the dramatic form. For we are meant to see the subject 'as a symbol of the part which is played in the general human lot by hereditary conditions in the largest sense'.[12]

Heredity is a form of bondage which George Eliot occasionally uses as a Fate in her novels. Here, she regards it as the feature

most distinguishing her tragedy from Greek tragedy. She hopes
to create 'a subject grander than that of Iphigenia',[13] grander
because the hereditary claim is acknowledged by the victim,
Fedalma, herself, however much she at first rebels against the
knowledge that she is Zarca's daughter, and must take his place
as Gypsy leader. Heredity is blood, that is nobility. For Fedalma
to reject her destiny is to reject her past – part of herself. To break
free would mean rootlessness, and pursuit by the Furies of the
conscience, representing the rightful claims of the past, as Maggie
Tulliver recognised. This is the fate of Don Silva,

> Close-baited by loud-barking thoughts
> Of that Supreme, the irreversible Past. (IV, 245)

The Spanish Gypsy is like *The Mill on the Floss* in that, unlike
the other novels, it presents this submission to the claims of the
larger life more equivocally. We are as aware of what is lost, and
its value, as of what is gained. There is no correct choice to be
made. Fedalma's feelings for both Zarca and Don Silva make it
impossible for her to be either the perfect daughter or the perfect
lover. The rejection of either bond involves a great wrong. There
can be no just conclusion to a clash between 'two irreconcilable
"oughts" '.[14] The tragic ending is terrible, rather than just, for
the punishment becomes disproportionate to the crime, cancelling
out all guilt.

George Eliot told John Blackwood that the poem would be less
tragic than she had threatened to make it, meaning that the lovers
would live. After reading Book IV, however, Blackwood was
understandably puzzled as to what kind of ending could in any
way alleviate what has so far occurred. Fedalma has already made
it plain that living without love will be harder for her than dying.
The ending, therefore, marks a return to George Eliot's usual
vision of tragedy. The divergence into heroic tragedy is not as
complete as would at first appear.

Felix Holt was written at about the same time as *The Spanish
Gypsy, Daniel Deronda* not until nine years later. But in both

novels George Eliot presents traditional concepts of heroism similar to those found in the poem, rather than the redefined heroism of the earlier novels. Although not born to command, the inner qualities of Felix Holt and Daniel Deronda make them natural leaders.

The two heroes recognise that a man with a strong will and personality can unify a mass of people and articulate their aims. Believing that the best of the group is needed to raise the class as a whole, rather than to seek his own advancement out of it, they determine to acknowledge and remain loyal to their origins, like Hardy's 'Native', Clym Yeobright. But the benefits are not one-way. The hero needs some ideal task, needs to feel himself 'the heart and brain of a multitude – some social captainship', (*Daniel Deronda*, III, p. 315) to prevent his heroic qualities destroying him through frustration. Each is able to put his beliefs into practice. Brought up as Sir Hugo Mallinger's nephew, but ignorant of his real origins, Daniel urgently needs to identify himself with a section of society that has a definite purpose. This will provide him with a role. The Jewish cause provides for him, as the working-classes provide for Felix, a specific focus for the heroic urge to lead and change the environment. For 'the fuller nature desires to be an agent, to create, and not merely to look on' (II, 301).

But in these novels, in contrast to *The Spanish Gypsy*, the heroic is not tragic. Fedalma's tragedy lies in the conflict between love and duty; in these two novels, love follows the direction of the heroic impulse, the hero's faith to the group. Mirah Lapidoth is not only Daniel's beloved, but a perfect embodiment of Jewry. And after her spiritual education, Esther Lyon comes to embody Felix's ideal of the noble beauty who would make 'a man's passion for her rush in one current with all the great aims of his life' (*Felix Holt*, I, p. 173). The individual is not required to make any real sacrifice for his people, although he may be genuinely prepared to do so. Felix and Daniel are finally able to pursue their ideals with the women they love.

In spite, therefore, of the emphasis on the actively, nobly

heroic, George Eliot's characteristic concept of tragedy remains unchanged in these novels. For the satisfying life is contrasted with the private tragedy of the isolated individual unable to satisfy his aspirations, with the fate of the many denied those opportunities which save Felix and Daniel from desperate frustration. The world of high society fosters the same pathetic tragedies that are found in the earlier novels of working-class life. Here too tragedy results from narrow circumstances, or from self-destructive egoism. In contrast to Daniel Deronda, Gwendolen Harleth suffers from a lack of motive which makes life dreary; the ties of the past are unimportant to her, and her rootlessness deprives her of even the earliest ready-made sympathies with the wider world. Her belief that her actions are of no consequence to anyone adds to her feeling of exile in the world. Solitude in any wide scene impresses her 'with an undefined feeling of immeasurable existence aloof from her, in the midst of which she was helplessly incapable of asserting herself' (*Daniel Deronda*, i, p. 90). Unable to associate with anyone or anything, she must dominate, but this desire makes her the wife of a man whose egoism is even greater than her own. She then suffers the humiliation of being subjected to his indifference. Gwendolen is another Mrs Transome, 'the pitiable woman who has once made herself secretly dependent on a man who is beneath her in feeling' (*Felix Holt*, i, p. 173). If a woman chooses moral mediocrity, her whole life takes on that pathetic colour.

These private tragedies highlight the contrast between the pathetic and the heroic. The contrast is also significantly between women and men, between Mrs Transome and Gwendolen on the one hand, and Felix and Daniel on the other. Denied those spheres of action open to men, women find heroism and fulfilment impossible. Esther Lyon defends the lack of enthusiasm women seem to have for men's ideals on the grounds that 'a woman can hardly ever choose in that way; she is dependent on what happens to her. She must take meaner things, because only meaner things are within her reach' (ii, 43). Mrs. Transome's sufferings become tragic when her son's return to Transome Court deprives her of her authority and function as acting head of the estate. She has become unsuited for the traditional passive role of women: 'life would have little meaning for her if she were to be gently thrust aside as a harmless elderly woman' (1, 22–3). In spite of their titles, these novels gain most of their impact from the central female characters, from their tragedies. The domestic situation convinces more than the heroic drama.

Despite this divergence into the realms of the heroic, therefore, George Eliot's predominant mode is that of pathetic tragedy. Her avowed intention to use the novel to convey a realistic and con-temporary tragic experience makes it impossible for her to ac-commodate within this form the grand, heroic tragedy which may still have a place in drama and poetry. That inarticulate, passive experience which is central to her conception of pathetic tragedy is, in turn, unsuited to traditional dramatic forms. Because the themes of her modern tragedy are distinct from those of tradi-tional tragedy, then the forms must likewise be different. Trying to convey an original – and to many readers, uncongenial – ver-sion of tragedy, she requires a form which allows for authorial intervention and explication. She shares H.G. Wells' view that 'the drama excites our sympathies intensely, but. . .is far too objec-tive a medium to widen them appreciably'.[15]

(v) GEORGE ELIOT AND THOMAS HARDY: A CONTRAST

George Eliot's vision of modern tragedy can be more clearly de-fined and appreciated in comparison with Hardy's use of tradi-tional tragic themes. Where Hardy sees life itself as a tragedy, George Eliot sees tragedy as part of life, but only a part. She takes us beyond tragedy. And where Hardy's novels show the formal influence of tragedy, George Eliot's show her fidelity to the realis-tic conventions of the Victorian novel. As a mode of continuity, the novel for her reflects the unending connections of human life, framing the tragic; Hardy's novels are dominated by the form of tragedy, which isolates the tragic pattern. Connection characterises George Eliot's vision as isolation characterises Hardy's.

Although George Eliot's fictional world is potentially tragic, she has confidence in man's ability to overcome at least some of life's hardships. The sense of outer forces dominates Hardy's novels, whereas it is the will, or the lack of it, on which George Eliot lays most stress. Chance, which takes away choice from Hardy's characters, forces moral choice on George Eliot's, bringing implicit moral attitudes into the open. Behind Tess's seduction the reader sees not only her inherited beauty and dreaminess, but economic conditions, family pressures, and the opportune arrival of Alec during her quarrel with the Queen of Spades. She falls suddenly and completely. Hetty's seduction is, in contrast, the culmination of a series of meetings, of several opportunities for retreat on either side. Insisting on the power of the will, George Eliot gives less weight than Hardy to the individual's unfulfilled aspirations: 'the final test of completeness seems to be a security of distinction between what we have professed and what we have done' (*Impressions of Theophrastus Such*, p. 193).

Such faith in the will implies a way out of tragedy, the possibility of a second chance. The structure of *Adam Bede* suggests that the individual can halt the tragic cycle, preventing the pattern from being repeated. Meeting for the second time at the Hermitage, where Adam and Arthur once fought over Hetty, the two men come close to their previous discord, but by sheer will-power disaster is averted. Hardy's characters rarely have such power, once the tragic mechanism has been triggered off. The alternative is only present in the terrible sense of waste, of what might have been. George Eliot hints at this occasionally: Gwendolen Harleth becomes 'a banished soul – beholding a possible life which she had sinned herself away from'. But the reader's attention is directed more towards Daniel Deronda's promising future, and to the possibility he raises of a new life even for Gwendolen, if she can think of sorrow 'not as the spoiling of [her] life, but as a preparation for it'.[16] The youthfulness which in Hardy adds to the poignancy of defeat makes recuperation possible in George Eliot's world, for she believes that 'it is but once that we can know our worst sorrows' (*Romola*, II, p. 443). For Hardy, as long as life continues, worse follows worse: as in *King Lear*,

> The worst is not
> So long as we can say, 'This is the worst'. (IV, i, 27)

George Eliot suggests that the tragic conflict can be resolved if faced. Her view of human life is progressive, whereas Hardy's is cyclical.

George Eliot's belief in the individual's ability to learn from his suffering suggests the traditional pattern of rebirth following tragedy. This is the truth that is inherent for her in the myth of the Resurrection. But her novels depict this recovery far more explicitly and fully than most tragedies. Adam Bede's sorrow, 'passing from pain into sympathy', (II, 302) prepares him for the happy family life shown in the last chapter, as does Daniel Deronda's. But the tragic knowledge that Michael Henchard attains dies with him. Even if the community simultaneously passes into a new stability, the tragic hero cannot live with his knowledge. In *Middlemarch*, George Eliot writes that, if we were fully aware of the sufferings of ordinary human life, 'we should die of that roar which lies on the other side of silence', but her own characters seem to remain reasonably 'well wadded' (p. 191), shielded from the blackness of this vision. The traditional tragic hero is also unable to live with other people. An outcast, isolated by what he has done, he becomes spiritually isolated by what he has learnt. He is also set apart by his passions, which Hardy isolates as the dominant force in the hero's being. It is their transfiguration by passion that takes his victims out of the realm of the pathetic and into the nobly tragic. The passions of Hardy's characters may not overcome circumstance, but they survive it, and are equal to it. They are fated and fateful. But for George Eliot, duty can and must conquer passion. Even Maggie Tulliver returns from her temporary submission to her passion for Stephen.

G.H. Lewes described tragedy as 'passion manifest in action',[17] but we rarely see passion in action on any significant scale in George Eliot's novels. She concentrates on how it can be controlled. Her approach is remedial, not tragic.

George Eliot's heroes can, in fact, return to society, once they have been purged by suffering. Her novels are less of an indictment of society than Hardy's are, because society as she sees it can accommodate the hero. And for her, the community is more important than the individual; co-operation is a greater ideal than individualism, however emotionally attracted she may be by the latter. Self-interest and the interest of the community are ultimately identical, for the individual is too involved in society to escape being hurt by what hurts society. George Eliot seeks meaning in terms of justice and community, rather than in personal affirmation, where Hardy finds it. The cost of returning to the community – even if possible – would be too great for Hardy's heroes, if it meant abandoning their desire for personal fulfilment. George Eliot tells us of men's duties, Hardy of their rights.

The suffering of George Eliot's characters is further alleviated by a poetic justice given the ultimate sanction of a Christian framework. The world of Hardy's novels is what Wordsworth calls

> the place where in the end,
> We find our happiness, or not at all.
>
> (*The Prelude*, Bk x, pp. 143–4.)

There is no forgiveness and no compensation in this unredeemed universe. As in the world of Greek tragedy, or in that of the Old Testament, there is no afterlife to compensate for earthly injustice. The natural law is not concerned with justifying its ways to men, but with making men acknowledge its power. The Christian background to George Eliot's novels denies the finality of death and the brevity of man's chance for happiness, although her personal writings show that she was acutely conscious of both. In her essay on Dr Cumming, she suggests that pity and love cease to be admirable when they are acts of obedience to God's will, in hope of life everlasting.[18] In the novels, the tragic tension is weakened because the reader is denied the impact of that courageous faith that clings to the ideal in spite of a reality which rewards selfish materialism.

But if the tragic vision conveyed in George Eliot's non-fiction appears to be compromised in her fiction, we need to recognise that this is not an accidental flaw in her work, but part of her intention. For in her work, just as the individual is re-absorbed into the community, so tragedy is absorbed into the novel. By taking the reader on to see what happens after the crisis, she concentrates on the gain, not on the loss. The seduction and death of Hetty Sorrel are used as a mere part of Adam Bede's story; Tess Durbeyfield's seduction and death are the whole story. What follows Tess's death seems unimportant. A mere hint of the future for Angel and Tess's sister, Liza-lu, is sufficient. To say more would seem a lack of taste and show lack of respect for the dead. In *Adam Bede*, however, our interest has always been with Adam and the community of Hayslope. Hetty's departure from the scene is not, therefore, meant to end our involvement. George Eliot is concerned with the consequences of her experience for family, friends and neighbours. The reader may share Henry James's feeling that, in the presence of Hetty's sorrow, no one else can lay claim to our interest, that 'in the presence of that misfortune no one else, assuredly, has a right to claim dramatic preeminence'. But James is criticising just that avoidance of tragedy upon which George Eliot is intent. Wishing that the story had ended 'with Hetty's execution, or even with her reprieve' and that 'Adam had been left to his grief, and Dinah Morris to the enjoyment of that distinguished celibacy', he desires the grand, final gesture. His insistence that Hetty is the central character in the novel ignores George Eliot's purpose. In spite of its title, the novel has no central character. In believing that Adam's marriage is 'matter for a new story',[19] James fails to perceive the real unity to which the novel aspires. The significance of George Eliot's handling of tragic themes and events is that her work shows them contained, both by life and by the form of the novel, which mirrors the continuity of that life. In Hardy's novels, we find that isolation of the tragic experience which characterises tragic drama. The urgency of the present and the finality of the action for the protagonists excludes all thought of a better future. Attention is unremittingly focused on the 'single opportunity of existence ever vouchsafed...by an unsympathetic First Cause', the victim's 'every and only chance' (*Tess of the D'Urbervilles*, p. 199).

The form of tragedy is, in fact, essentially alien to George Eliot's conception of the realistic novel. Any sense of crisis is overcome by the greater sense of continuity, so that there can be no real finality in any event. The structure of her novels suggests, within the bounds of the microcosm, the endless possibilities of relationship and interaction. The first four chapters of *Adam Bede* show the Bede family in the different contexts of work, religion, love, and the home, suggesting also the relationships between these spheres. Among the higher ranks of society, the author shows the same inter-relations, as she shows, too, the inter-action between the different social strata. As the novel proceeds, relationships are seen to be ever more complex, both in terms of people and in terms of interests. Most of the movement in George Eliot's novels is contained within this community network. The plot is forwarded primarily by action and reaction among its members. The plot of *Felix Holt*, for instance, is forwarded by a series of interviews, attempts to influence, persuade or dominate others, which reflect the different forms of political activity – 'treating', speeches and violence – by which society, like the individual's life, is shaped. The striking exception to this pattern is in *Adam Bede* – Hetty's journey out of the community. Like Hardy's three greatest tragic figures, she incarnates what is else-where only an image. Tess, Jude and Henchard are frequently seen on the road, seeking a new future and an escape. Centring on the story of an individual, each of these three novels follows his progress to the end, and shows the linear plot-structure typical of tragedy. Easily isolated, such a story-line gives the essence of

the work far more satisfactorily than would that of one of George
Eliot's novels. In the complex of stories which forms each of her
novels, events are less important than the processes of human
relationships which are almost as imperceptible as the grass
growing.

George Eliot's insistence on returning to the ordinary routines
of life that follow the crisis is a sign of her faithfulness to the
everyday basis of the realistic novel. Or, at least, it appears to be
intended as such. But do the endings of her novels really fulfil the
ideal of faithfulness to life? The need to resolve the novel's action
at some point inevitably clashes with her insistence on the complexity and endless connections of life, but it is debatable whether
the novelist is any less scrupulous in ending on a moment of high
tragedy than on an apparently static situation of domestic contentment. The Epilogue of *Adam Bede* provides a complete resolution of events. The action is rounded off and unified by Dinah's
words, 'Come in, Adam, and rest; it has been a hard day for thee'
(II, 379), words which suggest that Adam is now to reap the
harvest of his years of struggle. The Finale of *Middlemarch* also
ties up all loose ends, presenting a kind of tableau which is completely contrary to the dynamic complexity of the rest of the novel.
The implication is that nothing of importance will ever happen to
the characters again. The continuity and complexity of life is far
more successfully reflected in the notorious 'unfinished' endings
of Henry James's novels, which also achieve the sense of *stasis*
and resolution characteristic of tragedy. George Eliot may intend
the reader to feel that life has once more settled into its usual
rhythm, but rhythm is less evident than arrest.

The contrast between the themes of connection and isolation
in the work of George Eliot and Hardy respectively reflects the
differences between the characteristic methods and conventions of
the realistic novel and tragic drama. Tragedy is a formal influence,
as well as a philosophical one, on Hardy's novels. But for George
Eliot, it is primarily a moral influence confirming her own vision
of life and suggesting an ideal of responsibility for the novel;

Realism remains the predominant formal influence. The tragic experience is absorbed into her novels, connected with the currents of everyday life. But its supreme importance is in its potential impact on the moral development of humanity. George Eliot's mature work is a statement of faith in the wisdom and compassion which derive from tragic suffering.

5

THOMAS HARDY: TRAGEDY ANCIENT AND MODERN

(i) TRAGEDY AS A FORMAL CONCEPT IN HARDY'S NOVELS

It may be put thus in brief: a tragedy exhibits a state of things in the life of an individual which unavoidably causes some natural aim or desire of his to end in a catastrophe when carried out.   (*Early Life*, p. 230.)

Hardy defines tragedy in relation to the principle of *peripeteia* or reversal. Aristotle regarded *peripeteia* as one of drama's most important sources of emotional interest, and an important source of irony. The reversal is commonly highlighted in a 'recognition scene', in which the tragic hero is brought face to face with the past he tried to escape. The principle therefore superimposes a cyclical pattern on the hero's forward progress. After the birth and death of her illegitimate child, the offspring of her seduction by Alec D'Urberville, Tess finds hope in the seasonal renewal of life, and is inspired to go on in search of a better life by the belief that the past and its consequences would be swallowed up with the passage of time. But she forgets that this natural rhythm is cyclical. The 'phase' of the novel called 'the Consequence' shows her suffering to be a consequence not only of her seduction, but of her father's vainglorious attempts to reclaim his former aristocratic ancestry, and even of distant D'Urberville history. The structure of tragedy emphasises that 'our evil actions do not remain isolated in the past, waiting only to be reversed: like locomotive plants they spread and re-root, till to destroy the original stem has no material effect in killing them'.[1] The cyclical pattern reflects the interaction of past and present. The ironic reversals that result from the protagonist's ignorance of this interaction provide a structural equivalent of the tragic paradox expressed by St Paul in his letter to the Romans: 'the good that I would, that I do not: but the evil which I would not, that I do' (vii. 19).

Both the cyclical vision of life and the cyclical structure are underlined by the relationship between the beginning and the end of tragedy. During the course of Hardy's tragic novels, the imagery makes the reader increasingly aware of what the end must be, as the allusions to water and drowning do in *The Mill on the Floss*. Hardy's tragic heroes rarely regret their past actions; but they frequently regret ever having been born. Life itself is, it seems, their *hamartia*. Death therefore, is the only appropriate end for them – the only solution to the tragedy of being born on what Tess calls 'a blighted star'. Tragedy traditionally provides the double fate of life *and* death which reproduces the organic movement of life. Tess becomes poignantly aware that each year the most important date of all passes by without her knowledge: it is the date of her death, 'a day which lay sly and unseen among all the other days of the year, giving no sign or sound when she annually passed over it; but not the less surely there' (*Tess of the D'Urbervilles*, p. 125). Our awareness of this date's existence gives shape to life. In death the tragic status of Hardy's characters is completed. Eustacia Vye and Damon Wildeve, the unhappy illicit lovers of *The Return of the Native*, drown in the weir, the meeting place for their intended elopement. But here they finally achieve some of the romantic grandeur each so desperately sought and failed to find in life. 'Misfortune had struck them gracefully, cutting off their erratic histories with a catastrophic death, instead of...attenuating each life to an uninteresting meagreness' (p. 453). Here is the courageous tragic gesture frozen and made permanent by death. The essential is to die with dignity and at the right time: 'ripeness is all'. When the Mayor of Casterbridge dies, an impoverished outcast, he leaves behind him a will that is the finest affirmation of his integrity – 'a piece of the same stuff that his whole life was made of' (pp. 384–5). Dying in the conviction that it is time he troubled the world no longer, his 'testament' is a powerful and proud gesture of self-effacement. Tess's quiet acceptance of her arrest, and the inevitable price to be paid for her murder of her former seducer, arouses all the more awe and pity because it is not the acceptance of a failing, suffering body, but that of a life physically in its prime, and happier than at any time previous.

The influence of Aristotelian tragic theory on these novels is clearly seen in the relationship they assert between event and character. Hardy believed that the purpose of fiction was to gratify 'the love of the uncommon in human experience', as well as to give a lesson in life, and that 'the uncommonness must be in the events, not in the characters'. For him, as for Aristotle, the plot was the most important element. His are tragedies of situation, rather than of character. The titles of his four great tragic novels define the central characters by such 'situations' – 'the Native', 'the Mayor', 'the Obscure' and 'of the D'Urbervilles'. The conflict of ideas or feelings is made tragic by the situation. A comment from Hardy's diary throws light on Tess's murder of Alec: 'when a married woman who has a lover kills her husband, she does not really wish to kill the husband; she wishes to kill the situation'.[2] Any character defect or vulnerability in the protagonist may seem harmless until a particular situation arises; it may even have a certain value: Eustacia blames circumstances for making her undeniable charms a curse rather than a blessing. Hardy believed that individuals take, or are forced to take, a variety of roles upon themselves by the impact of circumstances upon each particular aspect of their character. Each character is largely a 'deeds-creature'. Tragedy arises out of the gap between what the character is – his true self – and what he does – the identity he presents to the outside world. In his concern for what happens to the hero, the reader makes contact with an experience related less to character than to forces which override it. In such tragedies, much of the pity and horror turns on the sense of wasted potential, the sense of individuals born in the wrong time or place.

If Hardy's concept of the best tragedy, of 'the WORTHY encompassed by the INEVITABLE',[3] is clearly Aristotelian, his theory of the novel shows a similar influence. It is based on those ideals of unity and organic structure by which the classical theorist differentiates tragedy from melodrama. 'Briefly, a story should be an organism' – quoting from Addison, Hardy continues, 'nothing should go before it, be intermixed with it, or follow after it, that is not related to it'.[4] The scenes of his novels are only completed by later scenes which bring out the significance of the earlier events. Unity is maintained by the unremitting focus on the central character and on those characters and events that directly affect him. The focus is intensified by the working out of the tragedy within the fictional world of Wessex. Although the characters move freely within this world, there is the sense of an enclosed arena, offering no escape from the tragic predicament. J. Hillis Miller explains this effect in the following way:

As he goes from one place toward another place the character is in the middle of the journey of his life. He is moving not just from one place to another, but from the completed past toward a future which has not yet come into existence. To express the temporality of human life in this way is to suggest covertly that the future already virtually exists, just as the past cannot fade from existence.

(*Thomas Hardy: Distance and Desire*, 1970, p. 201.)

These formal boundaries of place and interest prevent any distraction from the intensity of passion. Defending his use of a restricted geographical area, Hardy explicitly referred to Greek tragedy as his model.

In addition to showing these formal characteristics of tragedy, Hardy's tragic novels can be described more generally as dramatic. Hardy claimed that the 'portraiture of scenes in any way emotional or dramatic' is 'the highest province of fiction'.[5] As the Introduction suggested, this idea of uniting the ideals of drama and the novel was characteristic of the nineteenth century. Hardy himself gave the contemporary condition of the theatre and the decline of serious drama as his reasons for believing that the novel provided 'scope for getting nearer to the heart and meaning of things'.[6] In taking from drama the function of moral teacher, the novel also takes on many of its formal characteristics. Dickens provides another obvious example of this tendency, his novels borrowing from melodrama rather than from tragedy, from contemporary models rather than from ancient. But we find in his work, as in Hardy's, an essential structure of dialogue, action and stage-direction worked into a narrative continuity. And it is through dialogue and action that Hardy's characters convince, rather than through analysis. The sense of time in his novels is more dramatic than epic, internal rather than external, measured by the experience of the central character rather than by a clock or calendar: 'the number of their years may have adequately summed up Jared, Mahalaleel, and the rest of the antediluvians, but the age of modern man is to be measured by the intensity of his history' (*The Return of the Native*, p. 161). The reader is aware of the urgency of the present, of time running out, even when it passes slowly. Throughout the dreary and seemingly long, drawn-out period of Tess's stay at Flintcomb Ash, where she repeatedly reaches total exhaustion on the threshing machine, Alec D'Urberville is insistently present, waiting to offer help and make Tess his mistress again. Nowhere is the need for Angel Clare's immediate return from Brazil more urgently felt.

But Hardy is conscious that the revived presentation of high tragedy 'demands enrichment by further truths'. It demands original treatment, 'treatment which seeks to show Nature's unconsciousness not of essential laws, but of those laws framed merely as social expedients by humanity, without a basis in the heart of things; treatment which expresses the triumph of the crowd over the hero, of the commonplace majority over the exceptional few'.[7] With *The Return of the Native*, Hardy begins a series of experiments with tragic form. These experiments show how far his novels follow the traditional form of tragedy, and how far their forms result directly from the philosophy and experience they reflect. They represent the fruits of his search for an appropriate treatment of the 'further truths' the revival of tragedy required.

(ii) 'THE RETURN OF THE NATIVE'

In his study, *The Making of 'The Return of the Native'*, John Paterson points out that Hardy's first tragic novel began as a pastoral novel in the vein of *Far From the Madding Crowd*. But through a process of revision and growth, the novel underwent what Paterson calls a 'classical transvaluation' (p. 164). In this process it may also be that the possibilities of the novel as a tragic form evolved in Hardy's mind.

The most important change of emphasis Paterson describes relates to the heroine, Eustacia Vye – Romantic, well-educated and ladylike, ill-suited to the isolated life she shares with her grandfather, the old sea-captain, on Mistover Knap. Paterson shows how Hardy transforms her from a Satanic antagonist to an almost Promethean protagonist. The suggestions of supernatural evil are replaced by a portrait of human strength and frailty, made tragic by a natural environment of such power and influence as to almost appear a supernatural power. The melodrama of Wessex rural life takes on greater, more serious dimensions. The fire imagery, with its links with the Prometheus myth, and the classical allusions which evoke both the heroes and cosmic background of Greek drama, emphasise the classical, traditional nature of this tragedy of human aspirations. Characterisation has become more realistic, but is balanced by a network of imagery which frees the novel from the limitations of realism.

But what is the nature of the relationship between character and environment? Is the environment the source of the tragedy? The Heath thwarts Eustacia's aspirations to be queen of many hearts, for 'celestial imperiousness, love, wrath, and fervour had proved to be somewhat thrown away on netherward Egdon'.[8] But her unhappiness is largely due to her passivity before what she assumes is an unhappy Fate. And yet even this aspect of Eustacia's character cannot be isolated as the root cause of her tragedy, for her 'views on life were to some extent the natural begettings of her situation upon her nature' (p. 81). There is something, moreover, stronger than character. The fire imagery, the Heath and the water in which Eustacia and Wildeve drown, suggest elemental forces. The force of passion destroys the power of reason and finally destroys the individual himself. Love is linked with madness and death. 'A blaze of love, and extinction' (p. 79) is the greatest happiness Eustacia can hope for.

But there is an incongruity between the realistic material of the novel and the framework of tragic themes and imagery. This is most apparent when we look closely at Eustacia's aspirations. Her ambition to live in Budmouth, where her beauty and talents will be more appreciated, her passion for the ladykiller, Wildeve, and her rapid boredom with her husband Clym, the man of ideas, suggest the limitations of her intellect and imagination. She desires greatness, but does not know what greatness is. She burns with love, while painfully aware of the inadequacies of her lover. This transcendent emotion drives her to distraction for lack of a reality on which to focus it, a lack of what T.S. Eliot calls an 'objective correlative'. Her world offers no opportunity for the grand life-style and noble, super-human actions she associates with tragic heroines. It is this gap between the world of high tragedy and reality which is the source of her tragedy. For she creates a make-believe tragic world, a world in which the Turkish Knight she acts in the Mummers' play might really find a place. She creates a world in conspiracy against her, in order to provide sufficient excuse for her failure to achieve her ambitions. In her imagination, she turns the indifferent Egdon Heath into an antagonist. Unconsciously Eustacia seems aware – as Hardy is consciously aware – of the importance of place in tragedy, and of the grandeur she derives from her isolation on Egdon. If she had achieved her ambition of living in Budmouth, it 'might have completely demeaned her' (p. 79).

Her fatalism is to some extent an adopted stance. Compare, for instance, her educated self-alignment with the classical world with the deep-rooted paganism and superstition of rustics like Susan Nonsuch, whose feelings derive from the folk-myths they have inherited. The irony of Eustacia's make-believe is that she pursues those actions, such as her elopement, most likely to turn reality into an approximation of the hostile world her pride imagines. In trying to live out a role taken from ancient tragedy, she experiences the tragedy of modern life – the futility and insignificance of grand gestures in an indifferent universe.

Clym is continually aware of this real tragedy. His realisation that in this life 'there is nothing particularly great in its greatest walks' (p. 302), enables him to adapt to the humble work of furze-cutting, when failing eyesight prevents him from fulfilling his ambition of opening a school. He achieves a contentment of which Eustacia is jealous. And yet this apparently admirable stoicism, this wise modification of aims in the light of circumstance, is partly the result of the same impersonal forces of love and environment that drive Eustacia into defiance. In addition, the nature of Clym's original aims makes us question the worthiness of his submission to Fate. Eustacia's literary education leads her to visualise life as a heroic tragedy; Clym's education through suffering and experience leads him to realise the inadequacy of formal education to teach the individual to cope with tragic realities: 'I, who was going to teach people the higher secrets of happiness, did not know how to keep out of that gross misery which the most untaught are wise enough to avoid' (p. 371). But it is not this insight which leads him to abandon his idea of teaching; it is the pressure of his mother and wife, who seek to put him on a more materially ambitious path. His feeling that 'his scheme had somehow become glorified. A beautiful woman had been interwined with it' (p. 220) hints at his shifting priorities. The eclipse which heralds Wildeve's moving into Clym's shadow also heralds the gradual dimming of Clym's thirst for 'light', as well as of his sight, as it is overshadowed by the 'flamelike' soul of Eustacia, 'Queen of the night' (p. 75). His near-blindness links him with St Paul: he too abandons a prosperous and highly-respected position for the humbler role of teacher to the common man. But Eustacia's comment on this likeness is realistically ironic: 'the worst of it is that though Paul was excellent as a man in the Bible, he would hardly have done in real life' (p. 334). She believes Clym is out of touch with reality, yet she herself lives in a totally fictional world. The gulf between their worlds is fatal to their union.

This gulf reflects the discrepancy between the two concepts of tragedy with which Hardy seems to be juggling in this novel. The heroic tragedy of the exceptional individual, and what we may call the 'modern' idea of tragedy, inherent in life itself, are contrasted in the distinctive experiences of Eustacia and Clym. In superimposing images of classical tragedy onto a portrait of contemporary life, Hardy is working towards that vision of tragedy which finds its more complete expression in his later novels. Man suffers because he is everywhere unable to realise in modern life the image of greatness created by the poets and heroes of the past, and the aspirations fostered by the cruel, but powerful, delusion that he himself is the centre of the universe.

But the influence of tragedy does not enter the novel only on a thematic plane. Hardy originally planned to organise the novel into five books, like the five acts of Shakespearean tragedy, but this intention is lost in the novel as we now have it, for he was obliged to add a sixth book of 'Aftercourses' to satisfy his publisher's desire for a happy ending. The original ending, however, is more consistent with the tone of the rest of the novel, and satisfies what Hardy calls the more 'austere artistic code'.[9] Hardy accepts the traditional idea of death as the tragic ending in concluding Eustacia's story. In the weir she and Wildeve follow their passion through to its inevitable conclusion, at last submitting to the elemental forces which have been gradually destroying their integrity. But such an end is not for Clym. Like Lazarus, he experiences a kind of rebirth, returning to life fully aware of the horror of mortality, yet still longing for death as the only release from suffering. Is Clym too 'modern' a character for death? Is there a suggestion that the tragedy of modern life is not that men suffer and die, but that too often they suffer and survive, living greatly diminished lives? Or is the comparison of Clym with Eustacia simply a reflection of Hamlet's dilemma? Clym has not simply had a lucky escape: nobility finds its expression as often in passive fortitude as in active courage. Both elements seem to be present, for Hardy rarely adopts aspects of any tradition without absorbing them into his own vision of life.

Hardy's emphasis on unity of place, for instance, shows his recognition of the truth underlying the convention of the Unities – there is no escaping the tragic situation. Paris and Budmouth are frequently referred to as images of other worlds, but are always seen in terms of vague dreams. Eustacia's plan of escape leads her to the weir: death is the only exit. The title of the book suggests that each must fulfil his destiny against those surroundings which have formed him. This is above all a tragedy of place. All the complications are spatial. Each character is involved in the group arrangement, paired off in the way least likely to produce happiness, an image of the perversely ordered universe. Thomasin Yeobright marries Damon Wildeve, who loves Eustacia Vye, who marries Clem Yeobright, only to later return to her infatuation with Wildeve.

Similarly, there is no escape in time. The action of the tragedy covers a year and a day, if we exclude 'Aftercourses', as Hardy's footnote (p. 473) seems to authorise. There is little indication of life beyond either the beginning or the end. There is no significant interaction of past and present, and the future is another daydream, not a real possibility, to look forward to and prepare for. In spite of the constant activity and journeying to and fro on the heath, the novel therefore presents us with a suprisingly static and isolated moment in time. The heath provides a symbol of permanence, but it is a reminder of pre-history, rather than of the history of man.

It is this lack of extension in time that stands out if we try to see *The Return of the Native* as a formal and structural parallel to tragedy. The finality in the original ending of the novel makes it difficult to see the action as part of the flux and reflux of time, and therefore as part of the rhythm of sacrifice we associate with tragedy. We are not aware of any real renewal after the tragic experience, of order being re-established. The sixth book provides Thomasin and her child as representatives of the future and the continuity of life, but this new life seems too arbitrary and too abruptly 'given'. It does not suggest the painful extraction of wisdom and new strength from an experience of terror. Even leaving aside the irony in Hardy's description of the new life, the world of 'Aftercourses' seems too far removed from the rest of the novel to maintain the unity of the action and to be part of the tragic process. Tact dictates silence after Clym's famous 'great regret'. The experiences we are shown remain, therefore, largely private. Not only are the protagonists isolated as unique individuals; the tragic experience is not finally transformed into tragic order. This gap between feeling and form reflects, in fact, the novel's main theme – the inability of the tragically aware individual to give form and expression to his consciousness in significant action.

(iii) 'THE MAYOR OF CASTERBRIDGE'

The Mayor of Casterbridge is the novel most often used to demonstrate the influence of Greek tragedy on Hardy.[10] The sufferings of Michael Henchard are presented in the context of a strongly felt, if ambiguous, moral order and system of justice. The reader is particularly aware of this moral order because Henchard himself is so conscious of it, and of the evil nature of his impulses – 'these visitations of the devil'.[11] The intense focus on the conflicting moral impulses within a single figure provides Hardy with the means of expressing the tragic action in a form both as unified and as seemingly inevitable as that of Greek tragedy.

In describing the mayor as a 'man of character', Hardy seems to reject the idea of inevitability or Fate. The phrase suggests a self-wrought tragedy of the will. Yet our sense of an inexorable, all-powerful moral order is intensified through Henchard's experience of it as a force of opposition. It is always the man of will who is brought most vividly to realise his limitations and the strength of the power that rules the universe. *Hubris* and *hamartia* are inextricably linked. Elizabeth-Jane, whom Henchard at first believes to be his own daughter, has a fear of 'tempting Providence' which is justified by the succession of financial, personal and social disasters which begin to beset Henchard at the peak of his success. Even Henchard's far more cautious rival, Donald Farfrae, reaches a certain height, only to find his popularity declining as his power grows. Like character and environment in *The Return of the Native*, character and Fate are here intertwined or, rather, they are only two names for the same thing. How can character avail against circumstances, the 'lot' which Fate allocates, if character is not itself independent of Fate? Out of work, impoverished, and burdened with a wife and child, Henchard sells his wife and child in an attempt to escape his 'lot'. He frees himself of his family and poverty, but remains burdened with the impulsiveness of character which made him commit so desperate an act, and immediately regret it. Fate is no longer an external, but an internal, concept.

Henchard's actions are always out of touch with his deeper reasoning, because his instinctive drive and egotism triumph over his personal human needs. His desire to dominate, and his pride, alienate both Elizabeth-Jane and Farfrae, when he needs their affection. His desire for things of objective value – cash and status – blurs his understanding of love and friendship, distorting them into the desire for possession. Henchard's insistence on the fact that he had chosen Elizabeth-Jane's name reminds the reader of the primitive concept of naming as an act of possession. The clash between Henchard's will and his more human needs results in an ironic pattern of success and regret. Henchard achieves what he desires when he is least himself, or rather when he is least his better self. His regret at having rid himself of his wife is only the first of many such moments. After his fight with Farfrae, Henchard is subdued and ashamed: his 'womanliness sat tragically on a figure of so stern a piece of virility' (p. 316). His rational self is as helpless a victim of his violent emotions as are the women in his life. Only Abel Whittle, ill-treated when employed by Henchard, but grateful for Henchard's support of his ailing mother, penetrates to the core of loving-kindness in his employer. Like the typical wise fool of tragedy only he remains loyal to the end. Integrated within the individual, character and Fate are woven into a net from which death is the only escape.

Because Henchard cannot escape his character, he cannot escape his past. The actions intended to redeem the past are still the actions of the original offender. When his wife – after a separation of twenty years – traces him to Casterbridge, Henchard sends her five guineas, as if to buy her back. But he cannot buy back twenty years of accumulated conscience. And his action shows him again trying to treat human relationships as business transactions. The structure of the novel emphasises that his twenty years of atonement – of abstinence from the drink that caused his crime – merely postpone the punishment that always follows the crime. The whole period is passed over as we pass from the end of one chapter to the beginning of the next. His original desire to sever his human ties rebounds upon him. He is finally cast out from society. The return of the past, in the form of his wife and Elizabeth-Jane, triggers off the tragic mechanism.

This interaction of past and present, and the cyclical pattern of irony and reversal, distinguish the novel from *The Return of the Native*, linking it much more closely with Greek tragedy. The cycle of repetition is emphasised by the return of the furmity woman, who sold Henchard her doctored brew, and by the return of Newson, whose characterisation reiterates the suggestion that the intervening twenty years are as nothing:

The young sailor who had taken Susan Henchard on the spur of the moment and on the faith of a glance at her face, more than twenty years before, was still living and acting under the form of the grizzled traveller who had taken Henchard's words on trust so absolute as to shame him as he stood. (pp. 338–9)

Henchard himself becomes aware of this repetitive pattern, and his own behaviour is consequently modified. He goes to meet Lucetta Templeman, the woman he had promised to marry when he believed his first wife to be dead, intending revenge for Lucetta's having jilted him. But their meeting-place is the Ring. The memory of a past meeting in the same spot with his unhappy wife, now dead, fills him with compassion. This awareness grows out of his own sufferings, gradually increasing his sympathy and altruism. The development from egotism to self-effacement places the tragic experience within the rhythm of sacrifice. His departure from Casterbridge to a life of isolation and poverty shows his desire to remove his harmful presence from the only person he now cares for – Elizabeth-Jane. Hoping to offer her a wedding gift, he had instead received reproaches, which he had accepted in silence, where the reader has been used to violence, as the only outlet for the knowledge he has won, but is unable to express. In stoic endurance – expressed in his magnificent declaration – 'my punishment is *not* greater than I can bear' (p. 361) – Henchard finds expression for this tragic consciousness. His will and testament, the last expression of his powerful will, expresses a desire for self-effacement which, in terms of the rhythm of sacrifice, is pure altruism.

The cyclical pattern reminds us also of the mediaeval Wheel of Fortune, on which ambitious men never ceased from rising and falling. The image relates to the elements of chance and gambling on which Henchard relies so heavily, and to the Market, and the part it plays in his tragedy. The Market is the centre of Casterbridge life: everyone goes there for a living, however much he might prefer other means of negotiation. Human relationships are subordinate to the cash nexus. Such are the effects of civilisation.

But Henchard is himself involved in the processes of civilisation.

The unemployed hay-trusser rises to become mayor of a thriving market-town. His relationship, both real and symbolic, with Casterbridge suggests he is simultaneously hero and scapegoat. He represents the town as its first citizen, and also incarnates the clash in it between the primitive and the civilised. Mixen Lane, the 'mildewed leaf in the sturdy and flourishing Caster-bridge plant' (p. 244) is the town's guilty secret. This hiding-place for crime and discontent periodically disgorges its malice and barbarity in the open. The shock of seeing effigies of herself and Henchard paraded through the town in a traditional Skimming-ton Ride by these malcontents kills Lucetta Templeman. Violent passions lurk beneath the veneer of civilisation, just as in the mayor himself: 'though under a long reign of self-control he had become Mayor and churchwarden and what not, there was still the same unruly volcanic stuff beneath the rind of Michael Hen-chard as when he had sold his wife at Weydon Fair' (p. 129). The duality is emphasised by Casterbridge's Roman history, re-minding the reader that the great civilisation of Rome delighted in the bloodthirsty games that took place in the amphitheatre. The superstition in Henchard's 'fetishistic' nature emphasises the re-lationship between man and environment, giving realistic psycho-logical substance to Hardy's symbolism. Henchard's decision to drown himself is reversed by the sight of the effigy in the water, which seems to him an 'appalling miracle' (p. 342). This moment marks both the end of social disorder and the beginning of Hen-chard's spiritual regeneration. Social order results from private suffering. The marriage of Elizabeth-Jane and Farfrae, the in-heritors of both the old order and the new, recalls the union of the white rose and the red.

These relationships between Henchard and his society, and between past and present, assert the continuity of all experience, in space and in time, both public and private. Each action has wide significance because of its diffusive nature. In turn, the indi-vidual is extremely vulnerable to the movements of time and society around him. Henchard's fortunes rise and fall with the fortunes of the corn trade. His life is judged and given perspective by his relationship to these external factors. In Henchard, innocence and guilt are kept in balance: his intrinsically admirable qualities are corrupted by their sheer inappropriateness to the conditions of civilised life. His desire to come into the community is ultimately self-destructive. In Henchard's defeat, the reader is made aware of both the value of what is lost, and the rightness of the loss itself. The expression of this totality of experience makes possible a total tragic vision. In *The Mayor of Casterbridge*, the tragic vision and experience are worked into tragic order. The novel represents Hardy's first successful attempt to create tragedy – with all the formal implications of the term – in the novel.

(iv) 'TESS OF THE D'URBERVILLES'

'If way to the Better there be, it exacts a full look at the Worst'.[12] There are two complementary movements in *Tess*, related to each other by this belief. The external action taking Tess into painful isolation, and the internal progression from fantasy to reality, are linked by the Aeschylean belief that

> justice so moves that those only learn who suffer.[13]

The tragic action only achieves its final upward movement through this recognition.

We must distinguish between the physical degradation and the spiritual regeneration, and yet also see the link between them, in order to understand the tragic nature of Tess's experience. For her 'passing corporeal blight had been her mental harvest'.[14] Neither her lovers nor the society which Hardy postulates within and beyond the novel have this understanding. *Too Late Beloved*, one of the novel's provisional titles, is an ironic comment on the arbitrary and partial nature of their judgments. Because Tess accepts the false images others have of her, she is extremely vulnerable to the dreams and illusions with which she is tested along the 'long and stony highway' (p. 106) of her journey. Her pil-

grimage in search of a better future leads her only to the awareness that her future is inseparable from the past she is trying to
escape.

Tess is born into a world which thrives on illusions: the
Durbeyfield family live on romantic visions of a return to their
former glory. And while criticising their castles in the air, and
their dreams of her marriage to the young squire, Tess inherits
the same weakness. She is also prone to a melodramatic view of
herself which increases her sense of guilt. Her family encourage
this, by regarding her as their potential saviour. Everything is
against her living as herself, for herself. After her day-dreaming
precipitates the horse, Prince's, disastrous death, Tess sees herself
as a murderess. This is not simply an ominous foreboding, but
typical of the melodrama which is to characterise the relationship
between Tess and Alec.

The very environment in which Tess meets Alec is alien and
artificial. The newness of the red-brick building, the 'fancy farm'
(p. 42), and even the falsity of the name D'Urberville, suggest the
illusory and unstable nature of Alec's world. He bears all the
marks of the villainous seducer of Victorian melodrama – the
black moustache, full lips, swarthy complexion and rolling eye.
Tess immediately falls under the spell of his charm, obeying 'like
one in a dream', as if drugged by the 'blue narcotic haze' (p.
47).[15] Her ignorance of life combines with her natural dreamy
passivity to make her seduction inevitable: 'there lay the pity of
it' (p. 91). But here Hardy breaks with the world of melodrama.
Rejecting the convention in which seduction is usually 'treated as
fatal to [the heroine's] part of protagonist, or at least as the vir-
tual ending of her enterprises and hopes' (preface p. xvii), Hardy
treats this as the moment from which Tess's heroism begins. He
avoids the seduction itself, not simply out of the discretion required by his reading public, but because all such moments of
climax are in themselves unimportant. What matters are their
consequences, how Tess succeeds in coping with the new situation. The whole truth is not simply that Tess has succumbed, but

that, because of her resilience, adaptability and independence, she breaks free of the man who mastered her body, and faces the harsh reality she brings upon herself with dignity and courage, although alone.[16] Physically stained, mentally she has progressed. Hardy's plea is 'let the truth be told – women do as a rule live through such humiliations, and regain their spirits' (p. 135). The melodramatic crisis and the return to mundane normality are juxtaposed to contrast illusion with reality.

But Tess's second chance of happiness merely repeats this pattern of illusion and reality. Tess again moves from the romantic dream of May to the bleakness of the Winter that must always follow. In keeping her past secret from all her new friends at Talbothays dairy, Tess again opts for illusion. The villain of melodrama is replaced by Angel Clare, the Romantic hero; the man of flesh is replaced by the man of spirit, Tess's fear and suspicion by her love, but at the end of it she is again 'a lonely woman with a basket and a bundle' (p. 347). Angel sees Tess as a 'visionary essence of woman' (p. 167): he calls her by the names of Greek goddesses, when she only wishes to be called Tess, to be loved for what she is. Angel desires the untouched physical being that Tess was before she met Alec. He forgets that he also loves the spiritual being that she has only become since then. 'The touch of the imperfect upon the would-be perfect' (p. 192) makes her whole personality attractive, not merely her appearance. His subsequent disillusionment is unnecessary, for 'there is enough poetry in life, after all the sweet romance has been abstracted, to make a sweet pattern'.[17] Again Tess succumbs, accepting the unreal role Angel creates for her even while aware of its falsity. Her marriage ceremony seems like a dream, so little does she feel it can be real and lasting. Angel is to her a visitant from that other world his name suggests.

We are prepared for the intrusion of reality by the laughter which greets stories of deception and bawdry at the farm, an ominous hint of Clare's later view of his marriage as a case rather 'for satirical laughter than for tragedy' (p. 298). But this response is inadequate. While Angel is able to intellectualise and to detach himself mentally from the situation, the reader remains emotionally with Tess as she again takes on the consequences, now including a burden of physical suffering, and goes on alone.

The final phase of the novel again repeats the pattern, but in reverse. The seasons change, but now from Winter to Summer, and the cycle is halted before Winter can return. As each man returns to Tess, he seems altered as a result of knowing her. Alec has suffered spiritually, and Angel physically – new areas of experience for each of them – and they now see Tess more truly, knowing she is 'a pure woman'. But their experiences remain unreal in comparison with Tess's suffering. Alec's 'jolly new idea' (p. 394) of turning preacher, the adjective suggesting an immature schoolboy adventure, is all too easily abandoned. And, in spite of its hardships, Brazil is so remote that it seems for Angel a means of escape from the tragic predicament and the lash of Necessity, which for Tess are inescapable. Although she becomes Alec's mistress, entering the artificial world of Sandbourne, and then submits passively to Angel's vague plans in their last idyllic days together, Tess never again actually succumbs to illusion. And she remains essentially alone, isolated by her experience and knowledge, and dominating the scene in moral terms. The unreality of external events in the last scenes of the novel highlights their metaphysical significance, a significance with which Tess – in that complete separation of body and spirit which preserves her purity – is in contact. The great stones of Stonehenge provide a symbol of permanence. Their message can be conveyed in those words of Marcus Aurelius which gave Hardy himself such comfort: 'this is the chief thing: Be not perturbed; for all things are according to the nature of the universal'.[18]

Tess's hard-won knowledge of the tragic cyclical pattern leads her to commit her only self-willed action – Alec's murder – as a ritual expiation of the past. It is a kind of suicide, aligning her with all the great tragic heroines prepared to die to save or avenge their honour. She is prepared for the ultimate passivity of death, which alone can end the cycle. Her murder gives her private experience public significance, exposing her to public judgement and revenge. Her death itself is a ritual execution, but the implications of sacrifice are even more evident in Tess's sleep upon the altar, where the sun's rays strike her. Tess's whole experience has been of suffering, yet she still believes in that loving-kindness without dogma or reward which makes her even now remember her sister, Liza-Lu, and hope for a better life and a better world for her 'spiritualised image' (p. 506).

But the implications of sacrifice only become meaningful if Tess's experience has universal, as well as public significance. This universality is conveyed to the reader by a complex of symbolism which relates Tess to both history and Nature. This novel is related to a specific time and place, but Hardy universalises these particulars even more successfully than in *The Mayor of Caster-bridge* or *Jude the Obscure*. For this specific time of change is related to the eternal rhythm of change and the specific place to the natural world, in such a way that the reader is less aware of what separates that world from his own than of what endures beneath the changing face of civilisation.

Tess is initially related to the past through the mysterious D'Urberville legend, an association which is extended by the legend of the White Hart of her historic birth-place. The May Day celebrations which introduce her to the reader relate her also to the system of Nature, both as a setting and as a universal order. These rites herald the triumph of new life over the old, but here they take on sinister implications. For Tess is associated with customs and a rural society which are survivals of an older order; the Clare brothers who watch the May Day dancers represent the intrusive influence of the modern world. Tess dances to her own downfall. Angel's failure to choose her as a partner acts as a ritual gesture, signifying the ultimate result of this casual moment. Located in this system of Nature and Necessity, Tess's experience seems part of a greater rhythm, a repetitive pattern linking past and present, the beginning and the end of the D'Urberville line:

'so do flux and reflux – the rhythm of change – alternate and persist in everything under the sun' (p. 448).

Both Alec and Angel associate Tess with Nature, but in clusters of images which reveal that their misunderstanding of her reflects their ignorance of the Natural order. With Alec, Tess seems a 'wild animal', to be tamed by 'the kiss of mastery' (pp. 64 and 65). Her spirit attracts him, but must be broken, like that of a fine horse. It is a 'taming of the shrew' without the comedy. Both Alec and Petruchio employ the same tactics with women as they would with a horse or falcon, a strange blend of brutality and kindness. When Alec finds Tess working at Flintcomb Ash, he waits until she is totally exhausted by the threshing-machine before offering help. He makes Tess a 'caged wretch': wild Nature becomes a household pet, its spirit broken, or at least suppressed until the opportunity for revenge presents itself. Angel, however, believes Tess is already tame: she is a 'domestic animal' in his eyes, perfectly at home at Talbothays, domesticated nature incarnate. In seeing her as a 'daughter of Nature', he forgets Nature's cruelty (p. 155). He forgets that Nature is destroyer as well as creator, for he has not yet learnt 'the serpent hisses where the sweet birds sing' (p. 96), that Paradise harbours the evil one. Both men are ignorant of the laws of Necessity, aliens to the Natural order to which Tess belongs.

Their attitude symbolises that of the new order to the old. When driven from her home, the 'hunted soul' (p. 352) is able to adapt to life in the Vale of the Great Dairies. The fertile new land encourages growth and new life. But on the harsher soil of Flintcomb Ash, suffering from the incursions of industrialisation, Tess's heroic struggle is first for freedom, and then for mere survival. She is finally driven out of her natural habitat to the strangeness of Sandbourne. 'The old order changeth' (p. 465). In Tess the old aristocratic principle briefly emerges again and dies. This Darwinian vision of life as an unrelenting struggle is reinforced by the image of the hunt. Beginning with the White Hart legend, this image culminates in Tess, 'the bled calf'

(p. 427), sleeping on the altar, there to be discovered by her pursuers. And as Tess, the woman, is hunted by man, so mankind is hunted by the 'gods' – whether it be by the laws of Necessity which ensure that punishment follows crime, or by a society all too eager to ensure that no one escapes this primitive jungle law. The 'sport' of the controversial 'President of the Immortals' is as malignant and frivolous as that described in the *King Lear* image quoted in the Preface:

> As flies to wanton boys are we to the gods:
> They kill us for their sport. (p. xix)

For in this novel, while woman may seem to be set apart from man as his natural antagonist, she becomes his spokesman – she becomes a symbol of mankind as a whole. Hardy's use of female characters has frequently been commented on. Writing on womanly caprice in *A Group of Noble Dames*, Lascelles Abercrombie notes 'how valuable this characteristic conception of female psychology is to Hardy's art'.

For this womanly caprice, with all its tragical result, becomes at last the very type of the impersonal, primal impulse of existence, driving forward all its various forms of embodiment, profoundly working even within their own natures to force them onward in the great fatal movement of the world, all irrespective of their conscious desires.

(*Thomas Hardy: A Critical Study*, 1912, p. 85.)

Hardy makes many of the same observations on a woman's physical, emotional and social nature as George Eliot. Like her he sees women as inevitably the victims of men and the society they dominate, in spite of their power to destroy men in their turn. Tess's physical and emotional womanliness are the qualities for which she is loved, but also the qualities for which she suffers. Being desired, she must pay the consequences of that desire. Being loved, she must love more, becoming totally dependent on the whims of her beloved. This vulnerability seems, for Hardy, implicit in the image of the milkmaid. Tess and the other Talbothays milkmaids are all reduced to the same helpless misery by their feelings for Angel. All differences between them, all their attempts at individuality, are 'abstracted by this passion, and each [is] but portion of one organism called sex' (p. 187). In love, Cleopatra herself is

> No more but e'en a woman, and commanded
> By such poor passion as the maid that milks
> And does the meanest chores.
>
> (Anthony and Cleopatra, iv, 15, 72)

In his hope that he will find spiritual refreshment and a new love of life in his relationship with an 'unspoiled' country girl, Angel's feeling has a vampire-like quality in it common to all Hardy's portraits of such pairings. As the one thrives, so the other must ultimately fail.

And yet such generalisations on the nature of women are at the root of the sexual tragedy. Men and women are unable to regard each other as anything but separate species. Because Angel sees Tess as a being apart, he sets higher standards for her than for himself, cruelly insisting that she conform to his ideal. He cannot see that their 'crimes' are equal. Tess must suffer the injustice of the manmade law: 'then shall the man be guiltless; but the woman shall bear her iniquity' (*Jude the Obscure*, p. 384). But the individual cannot be judged by the general. Tess is very much a woman; she is even more herself. 'Any woman' would have married Alec, but not Tess. Any woman of the world would have won round Angel, but not Tess. Yet when she is least like Eve, refusing 'women's weapons', she is accused of Eve's vices, suffering Angel's 'ebullition of bitterness against womankind in general' (p. 308). In protesting against the fact that all women must bear 'the penalty of the sex wherein they were moulded', (*Jude the Obscure*, p. 168) Hardy is not exclusively interested in women. He is insisting on the right of every individual to exist and be judged on his own terms.

But, although man is 'the other victim', his aspirations constantly thwarted by love, these ambitions are themselves usually denied women. They remind us that

man's love is of man's life a thing apart
'Tis woman's whole existence.
(Lord Byron, *Don Juan*, Canto I, st. 194.)

Woman herself is always the final victim. Men may escape her, but she cannot escape herself. The imagery emphasises that woman is rooted in the unchanging Natural order, suffering under 'cruel Nature's law' – 'once victim, always victim' (p. 423). Man, in contrast, belongs to the active, changing social order. Woman is always to some extent out of place in the rapidly changing society man creates: she is unable to adapt quickly enough to control her own situation.

Tess of the D'Urbervilles is, therefore, a typically female tragedy, as *Jude the Obscure* and *The Mayor of Casterbridge* are typically male tragedies. They are tragedies of rebellion and aspiration, of the desire to change life; Tess desires merely to maintain her integrity. The novel is the most horrifying statement of Hardy's tragic vision because of the modesty of her desires. Suffering through her helpless dependence on men, and the vulnerability of her sex, Tess evokes a pity which questions the nature of humanity, and ultimately of the universe itself. For just so does man suffer in his helplessness before Fate, and through the limitations of his mortality. Hardy's other tragic novels each show a particular form of the conflict of personal and impersonal; *Tess* is its simplest and most universal statement. In all these novels, Hardy repeatedly uses the image of the bird – the archetypal symbol of the soul – for women, suggesting that the woman's tragedy is a type of the tragedy of all human life. For 'all are caged birds; the only difference lies in the size of the cage'.[19]

(v) 'JUDE THE OBSCURE'

According to Albert Guerard, Jude is not a tragic hero, 'if only because he is a modern'.[20] The word 'hero' is used in its traditional sense, indicating a defiant, active individual who seeks to impose his will on the universe. Jude may dream of this, but never achieves it. But to suggest that modernity is incompatible with tragedy is to ignore what so many readers experience as they read *Jude the Obscure*. It is not enough to dismiss its aspirations to tragedy merely because it has less contact than Hardy's other novels with the classical ideal. New concepts of tragedy are perhaps necessary. For the novel deliberately questions the traditional concepts of law and character associated with classical tragedy in a way that points towards twentieth-century ideas of 'modern tragedy'.

Jude's history is the record of his struggles with various forms of law. Each 'Part' of the novel highlights his experience of their different aspects. At Marygreen, Jude collides with the law of Nature, in the form of Arabella Donne. This supreme law subdues the will to instinct, the spirit to the flesh, individuality to the impersonal sexual drive. Jude is attracted to Arabella 'in commonplace obedience to conjunctive orders from headquarters, unconsciously received by unfortunate men when the last intention of their lives is to be occupied with the feminine' (p. 43). The discrepancy between his dream of learning and his actual pursuits only strikes him 'for a short fleeting while, as by the light of a falling lamp one might momentarily see an inscription on a wall before being enshrouded in darkness' (p. 46). This Natural law makes men and women bitter antagonists:

Under the hedge which divided the field from a distant plantation girls had given themselves to lovers who would not turn their heads to look at them by the next harvest; and in that ancient cornfield many a man had made love-promises to a woman at whose voice he had trembled by the next seed-time after fulfilling them in the church adjoining. (p. 10)

But tragedy enters only with the intervention of social laws that turn 'the normal sex-impulses. . .into devilish gins' (p. 261). Jude's momentary submission to a 'new and transitory instinct' (p. 70) is turned into a life-long trap by the unwritten law that he must marry the 'wronged' woman, and by the written law which gives this act of reparation such binding and allegedly divine sanction. The 'letter' constantly petrifies the essentially spontaneous and ever-evolving spirit.

Although Jude's ambitions survive this initial set-back, his first reactions to the University of Christminster, his goal, are ominous: 'it seemed impossible that modern thought could house itself in such decrepit and superseded chambers' (p. 92). The original energising impulse which built the colleges for just such as Jude has disappeared. In its place is a rigid educational system, geared to a rigid social system, with no room for changing human needs. Jude's drunken recital of the creed in a public house illustrates the degradation to which he sinks because of being unable to develop his potential within the existing educational and social structures. It also shows his intellectual superiority to many of those privileged to a place within these structures. Class barriers are as insurmountable as the college walls dividing Jude from those with whom he feels he has so much in common.

But while questioning the justice of such class laws, Jude retains an orthodox sense of ultimate law, of right and wrong, feeling immense guilt at his growing love for his cousin Sue. Believing he can accommodate himself to the laws of the church, he redirects his aims towards religion. But at Melchester, as at Christminster, in the centre of religion as of learning, he is an outsider. The attraction the city's nearness to Sue has for him hints at the conflicts to come. Jude seems at first unaware that there is anything in his liberal relations with Sue to conflict with the Church's laws, but they lead to 'a growing impatience of faith' (p. 235). Like Tess, Jude believes in the spirit of the Sermon on the Mount, but there is no room for such 'crude loving-kindness' (p. 434) in the strict ethical code of the established church.

Having struggled unavailingly with the laws to which the majority are subject, Jude creates a law unto himself when he moves to Shaston. His words to Sue, 'your will is law to me' (p. 287), reveal his commitment to love, for which he abandons his ambitions. She has remained 'dear, free Sue Bridehead' (p. 227) in spite of her marriage: she believes that by renouncing the sexual relationship, by refusing to abandon herself to Nature's law, she preserves her individuality intact. But, in imposing her will on Jude, expecting him to set her wishes above his 'gratification' (p. 289), she ignores his individuality. She wants to 'ennoble some man to high aims' (p. 183), and destroys three very different men in the process. Jude, like the others, is too human for her 'law': he is a whole man, flesh and spirit. Yet his success in changing Sue's laws, as he is unable to change any of the others, brings but a brief period of happiness. Determined to live according to their own sense of right and wrong, the lovers seek a home 'at Aldbrickham and elsewhere', seeking refuge in the crowd, but always hounded out because they refuse to adapt their individual needs to the ways of the mass: they refuse to conform to the law of survival. But faced with the choice – accept the law or die – only Jude has the courage to cling to the truth they have so painfully acquired.

For Jude's experiences on returning to Christminster convince him that there is no meaningful law. His sense of an ultimate law wavers during his lifetime as he alternately associates and dissociates it with civic law. He finally comes to see all laws as the expression of the forces which everywhere constrict the individual, forcing him into conformity with no regard to his uniqueness: 'the letter killeth' (p. 469). Jude realises, like Sue and Hardy himself, that tragedy lies 'in the forced adaptation of human instincts to rusty and irksome moulds that do not fit them' (p. xi). But he discovers that it also results from every attempt to shape a course according to instinct instead. Law judges the individual by his actions, the 'identity' he presents to the outside world. Little notice is taken of the lifetime of extenuating circumstances represented by his aspirations. The reality is everything, the ideal, nothing. Jude is judged by the observed reality of his drunkenness, 'the regular stereotyped resource of the despairing worthless' (p. 82), and his illicit relationship with Sue, not by his unique and elevated motives. On the basis of such a judgement, society rejects him. And the sufferings they hurl upon him suggest that the powers that rule the universe uphold this judgement. In answer, Jude rejects their judgement in the only way he can, by rejecting the laws by which it was framed.

The void left by this rejection is terrifying. If the traditional tragic hero 'undertakes to break the laws in order to express the full dimension of human existence'[21] and if he then loses all belief in these laws, where is the significance of his action? However much the individual may wish to assert his uniqueness against the law's classifications – the divisions into innocent and guilty, respectable and disreputable, elect and damned – the resulting absence of any kind of definition or sense of relationship is paralysing. In contrast, Sue accepts divine law and so gives meaning to her suffering. In accepting suffering as a punishment for her sins she finds a kind of escape. Her acts of atonement provide an outlet for anguish which is denied Jude. Although he answers Sue's 'it is no use fighting against God' with the assertion that 'it is only against man and senseless circumstance' (p. 413), he himself is unable to act to change society; he can only dream. Constantly matching his self against his 'identity', his ideal life with the reality, he remains passive, caught between the vision of himself that his ambitions tell him he can be, and the suspicion that his real destiny is with the workers. He is too involved with trying to define himself in a void to be able to live. The sense of waste is overwhelming.

Character is here clearly more problematic and modern in concept than in Hardy's earlier novels. Because action is no longer purposeful, the author cannot rely on this alone to convey character. He must convey the clash of irrational impulses behind the action, for the tragedy centres less on fateful action than on inner torment. But although *Jude the Obscure* focuses on modern experience and modern man, this does not make the suffering it represents local and temporary. Hardy uses the details of contemporary law and society as 'particulars containing a good deal that (is) universal, and not without hope that certain cathartic, Aristotelian qualities might be found therein' (preface p. x). The laws are seen as an expression of the feelings of collective man, of the innate injustice in man's nature. The contrast between the social shapes which characters are fitted into and their true nature gives weight both to the society Hardy depicts and to that in man which is asocial and therefore unchanging.

But the 'cathartic, Aristotelian qualities' are few. Jude and Sue are completely isolated by their attitudes, except perhaps briefly from the schoolteacher Phillotson. Although they 'have wronged no man, corrupted no man, defrauded no man' (p. 371), they seem to be fighting the rest of mankind, who represent those laws they reject. The split between the private and the public is complete. There is none of the representative relationship between the hero and society, or even a section of society, that we find in *The Mayor of Casterbridge* and *Tess of the D'Urbervilles*. Jude and Sue speak not for a race that is dying, but for a race that is yet to be born. Jude remains an outsider to the end of his days. Raymond Williams has suggested that, in modern tragedy, the rhythm of sacrifice no longer exists in its original form: 'our emotional commitment. . .is to the man who dies, rather than to the action in which he dies. At this point a new rhythm of tragedy enters, and the ceremony of sacrifice is drowned, not in blood but in pity'. The beginnings of this process are present in all Hardy's tragic novels, but in *Jude* it is taken to its limits. Jude, the conscious individual, dies, as it were, to save an inconscient world. Tragedy lies not only in his sacrifice, but to quote Williams again, 'in the general condition, of a people reducing or destroying itself because it is not conscious of its true condition. The tragedy is not in the death, but in the life'.[22] Sue lives, but 'she's never found peace since she left his arms, and never will till she's as he is now' (p. 494). To the inconscient world Jude is only a failure: his sacrifice is misunderstood and unavailing. The novel leaves the reader not with the sense of a world saddened but wiser, not with a sense of order rising out of chaos, but with the harrowing and unreconciled cry of the martyred saints – 'How long?'[23]

If the individual perceives the utter absurdity of this unconscious universe, the only logical action would seem to be suicide. This is virtually the course Jude takes when he visits Sue for the last time. Endurance is no longer valuable or significant. The complete bleakness which comes from this recognition is emphasised by the form. Jude dies alone and abandoned. The novel ends at a point similar to that at which Angel leaves Tess in Sandbourne; there is none of the idyllic reconciliation that follows in the earlier novel. Jude is totally unreconciled both to his own life and to the world outside, whose hilarity during his moments of agony grotesquely heightens the sense of discord. His death is in no way distanced or ritualised to soften its impact. Henchard's death is narrated in Whittle's great elegy: the mayor takes himself 'offstage' to die, in the classical manner. Tess's death is ritualised by the preceding dream-like Stonehenge scene, and again her death is not portrayed. But in Hardy's last novel, the classical tragic ending, 'calm of mind, all passion spent', is rejected for Jude's dying curse on life and the account of Sue's tormented soul. As in *The Return of the Native*, the tragic experience is not finally transformed into tragic order. Again this reflects the inability of the tragically aware individual to express his consciousness in significant action in the modern world. But in the later novel the discontinuity seems more conscious on Hardy's part. Here he follows his thoughts on life to the ultimately pessimistic conclusions: the whole cosmos, not the individual, is at fault. It is the sign of Jude's strength and Sue's weakness that he can, and she cannot, face this conclusion. In order for her to feel her children have not died in vain, the universe must be meaningful. She reasons like T. S. Eliot's Celia:

> . . .I should really *like* to think there's something wrong with me –
> Because, if there isn't, then there's something wrong,
> Or at least, very different from what it seemed to be,
> With the world itself – and that's much more frightening!
> That would be terrible.
>
> (*The Cocktail Party*, 1950, p. 117.)

And so it is in *Jude the Obscure*.

6

HENRY JAMES: FREEDOM AND FORM – THE TRAGIC CONFLICT AND THE NOVELIST'S DILEMMA

(i) TRAGEDY AND THE NOVEL

Like Hardy, James sees the 'unfulfilled intention'[1] everywhere. The central idea in his concept of tragedy is that of waste. The wasted potential may be presented in terms of specific artistic gifts or opportunities, but it always symbolises the boundless possibilities of human life. In each novel James repeats the demand made by Kate Croy in *The Wings of the Dove*: 'why should a set of people have been put in motion, on such a scale and with such an air of being equipped for a profitable journey, only to break down without an accident, to stretch themselves in the wayside dust without a reason?' (I, 4). The contrast between departure and breakdown suggests the same elements of irony and reversal that characterise the structure of Hardy's tragic novels. And yet, however clearly defined the pattern of tragedy may be in James's work, it does not dominate the form of his novels as it does Hardy's. James's novels are closer to George Eliot's in their mood, their complexity and their feeling for the continuity and interrelationships of human life. In order to give equal weight to both the traditional and contemporary ideas of tragedy with which he is concerned, he attempts to combine the relevant qualities of tragedy and the novel in the most appropriate measures.

If, therefore, James – like Hardy – frequently conforms to the pattern of traditional tragedy, ending with the hero's death, he equally often presents the alternative pattern of the tragic life, with its stress not on finality, but on continuity. The tragedy is not always that life is too short, but that the individual is unable or unwilling to lead that life to the full. The tragic situation may not be the result of character, but James is less ready than Hardy to exonerate the individual's reaction to that situation. What the individual makes of life depends on certain personal possibilities of circumstance or character. The particular opportunities he is given may fail to live up to his imagination and ambitions, but it is equally possible that his imagination fails to live up to the opportunity. What is ultimately wasted is not the individual and his talents, but life itself.

When opportunity fails to live up to the imagination, the temptation is to live too fast. This is typically the tragedy of the young. Life seems too short and too restricted, so that the individual endeavours to cram the maximum of experience into the limited scope available. He fails to take time to reflect, to evaluate what he is doing and why. There is no time to connect, to form relationships with potential for growth. Leaving the past behind in his haste, the individual becomes increasingly isolated. This happens to both Roderick Hudson and Christina Light. Roderick consumes pleasure at such a rate that he 'might have none left for the morrow'. Like Stendhal, he has 'seen too early in life *la beauté parfaite*'.[2] Left with only his imagination of it, he is unable to find or create the corresponding reality. He and Christina destroy themselves and their chances of happiness in pursuit of the world of their imagination. Milly Theale's situation, in *The Wings of the Dove*, is an exceptional example of this kind of 'burnt-out case'. Milly lives too fast by necessity, not by choice. Because her end is pre-determined by illness, she can make better, because more conscious, use of her limited time. But she too dies – we feel almost by choice – when her life no longer corresponds to her imagination of it.

Ralph Touchett, in *The Portrait of a Lady*, is also fatally ill, but his experience illustrates an alternative pattern of tragedy. He is one of those who can be said to never live at all, the starkest example being John Marcher, the hero of *The Beast in the Jungle* – '*the* man, to whom nothing on earth was to have happened'.[3]

Such characters fail to live because they try to live vicariously. Rowland Mallett only lives through Roderick Hudson, turning his back on any chance of happiness with Mary because of his friendship for her fiancé. Roderick is a mouthpiece for his frustrated 'need for expression'. The emptiness resulting from Roderick's death is inevitable: 'Now that all was over Rowland understood how up to the brim, for two years, his personal world had been filled. His occupation was gone'.[4] But Ralph cannot live fully because he is dying. For him vicarious living has, therefore, a more positive, moral value as an attempt to connect with that life he cannot personally share. He represents the Jamesian artist and the values of the detached, but not indifferent, stance. His is clearly not an instance of imagination failing to live up to opportunity. James constantly varies and adds further complexities to his treatment of these recurring themes.

The relationship between Kate Croy, Milly and Merton Densher provides James's most interesting variation on the theme of vicarious living. Densher charms Milly as a means to marrying Kate, hoping to benefit from Milly's riches enough to satisfy Kate's expectations of good living. Kate and Densher try to live not so much through another person, as after her. They fail, therefore, to realise present opportunities, continually projecting their imaginations into the future. Consequently, they miss their chance, and never really live at all. They fail, like those who use themselves up too soon, to realise that 'what you had most to do, under the discipline of life, or of death, was really to feel your situation as grave' (*The Wings of the Dove*, 1, p. 95). Each must finally come to terms with the fact that he has had 'the one chance that all men have – he had had the chance of life'.[5] There is no second chance. Stressing, like Hardy, the unique opportunity of earthly existence, James suggests the utter impossibility of recompense.

But in spite of this emphasis on the finality of death, continuity, or connection, is also given both a thematic and formal emphasis. 'Only connect' seems to be a principle for James and George

Eliot as much as for E.M. Forster. Tragedy derives from the absence of continuity, continuity of purpose and relationship. The individual is inextricably involved in the world of people and things. He needs to participate actively in that involvement, using it as a means of finding and asserting his identity. But the problem for James's heroes, as for Forster's, is to connect without sacrificing their freedom. And the novelist who wishes to convey this sense of connection and continuity is also faced with a problem. James describes it as the temptation offered by 'developments':

They are of the very essence of the novelist's process, and it is by their aid, fundamentally, that his idea takes form and lives...They are the very condition of interest...the painter's subject consisting ever, obviously, of the related state, to each other, of certain figures and things...Where, for the complete expression of one's subject, does a particular relation stop – giving way to some other not concerned in that expression? Really, universally, relations stop nowhere, and the exquisite problem of the artist is eternally but to draw, by a geometry of his own, the circle within which they shall happily *appear* to do so. (Preface to *Roderick Hudson*, pp. ix–x.)

The circle which James draws is often the full circle of tragedy. The tragic pattern isolates the subject, setting its own necessary limits. It controls the tendency to diffusiveness which made James so suspicious of 'simple' realism, of an apparently faithful rendering of life's clumsy work. He admired *Middlemarch*, but felt it set 'a limit...to the development of the old-fashioned English novel. Its diffusiveness...makes it too copious a dose of pure fiction'.[6] In his tragic novels, diffusiveness is held in check by an isolation at once thematic and formal. As in Hardy's novels, the tragic hero is isolated by his fate and by his nature. This isolation highlights the inequality of his struggle. The individual is doomed to lose because he is one and the opposition is many. Society observes Milly Theale as an audience observes 'the princess in a conventional tragedy'. With its 'involved loneliness and other mysteries' (*The Wings of the Dove*, i, p. 108) this image reflects the solemnity of the situation. The tragic journey is isolated by the exclusion of everything that is not relevant to the tragic situation, its cause and effects. James delights in economy. Like Hardy he believes that a novel should have organic form. If the novelist concentrates on the story, its beginning, its middle and its end, a logically organised form inevitably follows, for form and content are one. James's impulse is to 'make the first step of (the) situation place itself only exactly where that situation may be conceived as really beginning to show'.[7] Isabel's story begins with her entry into Europe; *The Wings of the Dove* begins where Kate learns to feel the embarrassments of poverty and the consequent temptations of wealth; *The Bostonians* opens with the fateful coming together of Basil, Olive and Verena. Any necessary background is provided in due course, but the prominent outline of events deals with the results of the new situation. The timescale is kept relatively brief so that the main events retain a vivid immediacy; in contrast, past history seems remote, as it feels to those plunged into the overwhelming demands of a strange present.

James's world is, therefore, in many ways isolated, giving little idea of the life of the working masses, or even of that work on which the wealth of the American travellers is founded. Even when the hero travels across the world on his journey of discovery, his own circle frequently travels with him. But within this enclosed world, there is movement and a sense of opening up, in terms of enlightenment. The structure and workings of the circle are revealed with increasing clarity. It is not so much that the 'underworld' is excluded by James's concentration on the upper classes, but that it is implicitly included. Whatever different forms the tragic obstacle to happiness may take, and under whatever different conditions the buried life may struggle, the basic concepts of Jamesian tragedy apply equally to all social classes. For James, 'art is essentially selection, but it is a selection whose main care is to be typical, to be inclusive'.[8] James's exclusive élite becomes typical because, through its isolation and the emphasis on the connections which hold it together, it stands as a microcosm, demonstrating the tragic law of 'the close connexion of bliss and bale, of the things that help with the things that hurt'.[9]

In James's tragic novels, two principles are at work – the principle of inclusiveness which belongs to the epic narrative tradition, and the principle of selection or isolation which belongs to the tradition of classical tragedy. The tension between them reflects the conflict which James is continually trying to resolve – the conflict between the novel's tendency towards total freedom, towards a complete reflection of the anarchic disorder of life, and the artist's desire to make of the novel a work of art, to impose on that chaos form and order. And this tension also mirrors the conflict that is the source of tragedy. The conflict for the Jamesian hero is between the desire for freedom, and the need – sometimes imposed from outside, but more often felt within – to adopt some kind of form. He needs some recognisable function to give his life direction, to provide shelter from the sometimes terrifying prospect of total freedom.

(ii) 'THE AMERICAN'

In *The American* James portrayed 'one of those insuperable difficulties which present themselves in people's lives and from which the only issue is by forfeiture'. It illustrated one of those 'tragedies in life' which, he confessed to W.D. Howells, the American novelist and critic, arrested his attention more than any other subject.[10] And yet, in spite of its tragic theme, the novel never achieves the tragic effect of *The Portrait of a Lady*, or *The Wings of the Dove*. James himself felt that the novel turned into a romance. But instead of seeing *The American* as a failure as tragedy, compared with the later major novels, we should see it as an expression of a peculiarly modern and characteristically Jamesian concept of tragedy. Together with what are often called the tragic novellas – *Washington Square* and *The Spoils of Poynton* – *The American* expresses ideas which are not rejected in the later novels, but assimilated. James's mature work absorbs these ideas into a synthesis of modern tragic themes with more classical ideas of form.

The obstacle to happiness for James's American hero, Christopher Newman, lies in the forms of European civilisation which prevent him marrying the woman he loves. Form is here seen as antipathetic to freedom: it is the tragic veto. Although the conflict between form and freedom is a recurrent theme in James's fiction, in this early work he seems less confident that there can be any viable relationship between the two. There is little sense of the value of form, such as we find in *The Portrait of a Lady*, *The Wing of the Dove* and *The Golden Bowl*, little sense that a resolution between freedom and form is not only possible, but desirable. Moral superiority and integrity can only be asserted – this novel implies – by a total rejection of form, but not before form itself has ruined the lives of those involved. Because form is seen in a negative light, its defeat of freedom carries with it no compensation. There is no suggestion of equilibrium, that loss is countered by gain, that the individual's sacrifice benefits the community.

The woman with whom Newman falls in love is Claire de Cintré, a widow, and daughter of an ancient and honourable family now finding its position, socially and financially, less secure than formerly. The family de Bellegarde adhere so rigidly to the code of honour and good form that they have become inward-looking and self-contained. Their home strikes Newman with its air of privacy and its 'impassive' face (p. 52). Unable to break out of the traditional mould, the individual members of the family are stifled. Valentin, the son, wants to extend himself like Newman. His eyes are 'completely void of introspection', and he is 'intensely alive' (p. 114). Yet his life is a conspicuous example of waste. He has done nothing but 'play the part of a gentilhomme'. Working, he feels, might make him seem 'a man who dominated circumstances' (p. 301), instead of one whose will has been neutralised by them. Claire's personality also has the potential for expansiveness. She is described in significantly American terms: she has a 'range of expression as delightfully vast as the wind-streaked, cloud-flecked distance on a Western prairie', in contrast to her mother's 'circumscribed smile', and face that suggests 'a document signed and sealed' (p. 161). In spite of her rigid background, she reverses the process undergone by Gilbert Osmond, who attempts to turn life into art: 'She looks like a statue that had failed as cold stone, resigned itself to its defects and come to life as flesh and blood' (p. 131). But when family pressures are brought to bear on her, she rapidly reverts to the statue-like, Newman noticing a new 'monastic rigidity in her dress', and her 'lifeless' touch (p. 357). Her identity has so often been sacrificed to the demands of her family that the only way she can find peace is by wilfully abandoning her identity, forcing herself into the even more rigid mould of convent life. Her name, the very symbol of identity, is the first thing to be cast aside.

But the living death of the convent is merely an extension of Claire's previous existence. Earlier in the novel Valentin, supporting Claire's decision to re-enter society after a prolonged mourning, argues that she has 'no right to bury herself alive' (p. 171). The image is to be repeated many times when she decides to take the veil: she pleads with Newman, 'let me bury myself. . .I'm afraid of my mother'.[11] She takes refuge in the strict order of the convent not because there is value in form, but because she has not the courage to fight. Form is a total retreat from life, a refuge from the pain and struggle involved in the fight to preserve one's freedom.

For form is an appearance divorced from reality, a ritual to conceal the ugliness on which such an apparently high degree of civilisation rests. It may have, in Valentin's words, 'a kind of picturesque charm' that is amusing in 'this age of vile prose', but the falsity becomes tragic when it extends to life-and-death issues. When Valentin engages in a duel, Newman picks up the literary image, telling Valentin that the duel of honour is nothing but 'a scene. . .It's a wretched theatrical affair' (p. 314). When the proprieties are observed, manslaughter becomes mere ritual – a bloodstain clears the stain from the family honour. It is violent speech, not action, that is intolerable. The de Bellegardes charge

Newman with 'violence' and 'roughness', because he insists on hearing, face to face, the reasons for their finally rejecting him as Claire's suitor. When he tells them that Valentin, dying from the wound received in the duel, apologised for their behaviour towards him, 'the effect of these words was as if he had struck a physical blow' (p. 378). Their violence is, in contrast, concealed by the smooth exterior. Even Claire is so imbued with the life-long practice of form, if not with the principle, that when she faces Newman for the last time, she presents a calm exterior which is the result of violent effort.

And yet Claire's formal upbringing is part of her attraction for Newman. She gives him the 'sense of an elaborate education, of her having passed through mysterious ceremonies and processes of culture in her youth, of her having been fashioned and made flexible to certain deep social needs' (p. 145). He is eager to observe all the formalities in his approach to her. The superficial attractiveness of form is, therefore, an important element in the plot, as well as contributing to the vigour and humour of the novel's tone. It is at one point even implied that it is not this formalistic society that is at fault, but the intrusion of outsiders into it. Ms Ledoux and Grosjoyaux claim that K killed Valentin in the duel precisely because he was a brewer's son, and therefore failed to understand the nature of duelling: a nobler man would have aimed to miss or merely to wound, as did Valentin himself. Form is seen as a coded means of communication. Among the initiated, all runs smoothly. But whether or not Newman would have been wiser to stick to his own kind, the de Bellegardes and their associates stand condemned at the most basic moral level, even in their attitude to each other. Newman's great error is to be too easily beguiled by form himself: he is all too ready to take exclusive possession of a wife, to amalgamate another individual's freedom into his own system. He is similarly tempted by revenge, as hollow and meaningless a form of action as the duel. But Newman has to learn to rely on his inner strength, on his private knowledge of having acted rightly, even when he has been cruelly wronged. There is no point in seeking symbols and proofs of it; even Fleda Vetch must learn to live without the solace that the possession of one of the beautiful Spoils of Poynton would have brought.

Initially, freedom – in the guise of Christopher Newman, representative of the New World – appears to challenge form. The idea of freedom is conveyed through positive, vigorous images – images of expansiveness that suggest growth and energy. Newmans' self-confidence is such that he can absorb the new European milieu without its throwing any doubts on his identity, or swaying his own judgement and standards. He is perhaps too confident, almost absurdly unaware of Europe making any intellectual or moral demands upon him. As an active businessman, Newman is a doer rather than a thinker, having as yet had little time for making himself felt emotionally or intellectually. His habit of stretching out his legs when sitting down, a 'symbol of his taking mental possession of a scene' (p. 101), expresses his physicality. His choice of apartments similarly reflects his expansive personality: his 'ideal of grandeur was a splendid façade, diffusing its brilliancy outward too, irradiating hospitality' (p. 52). But as Newman's power to free Mme de Cintré from the grip of her family proves less and less, his activity is increasingly reduced. He reaches that stage of inactivity which is typical of the 'free spirits' of the tragic novellas.

The renunciation James finally offers as the only means of freedom may be heroic, but it is hardly effective. It involves a withdrawal from life, rather than coming to grips with it, and therefore appears a far more negative concept than it becomes in the later novels. The only victories are inner victories. Newman is released from 'ineffectual desire' (p. 468) when he faces the irreversibility of his loss. He decides against exposing the skeleton in the de Bellegarde family cupboard – the probable murder of Claire's father. But his friend Mrs Tristram questions this renunciation. She suggests that the de Bellegardes only succeeded in keeping Newman away from Claire because they relied on Newman withdrawing his threat of exposure. He ought to have called their bluff. In safeguarding his own integrity, he has perhaps unnecessarily sacrificed the happiness of Claire and himself. His readiness to abdicate leaves the stronger and less moral in control, just as Fleda's passivity leaves Owen in the unscrupulous Mona Brigstock's grasp. Although Newman feels that, in entering the nunnery, Claire has 'moved off, like her brother Valentin' (p. 388), to give him room to work his revenge, he fails to take up the advantage of the family secret given him so painfully on Valentin's death-bed. Valentin himself, like Claire, is perhaps all too ready to retreat in the face of shame, or at any hint of conflict. Although his death-wound is real enough, his assertion, 'when my people – when my "race" – come to that, it is time for me to pass away' (p. 349), indicates a fatalism which abandons the world to the forces of evil. In the free spirit's struggle with the world and the will, we are more aware of paralysis and defeat than moral strength.

The limitations of freedom are perhaps deeply felt here, as in the tragic novellas, because of the lack of reverberation which the action or presence of the free spirit produces. *The Portrait of a Lady* ends with the sense of new beginnings, *The Wings of the Dove* with the sense that nothing will ever be the same for the survivors of Milly Theale's tragedy. But the witnesses in *The American* experience no awakening of the moral sense. Indeed, there are no real witnesses left to acknowledge Newman's sacrifice. Claire and Valentin are both silenced, and Mrs Tristram is ill-equipped to understand or appreciate his actions. Like Mrs Gereth in *The Spoils of Poynton*, and Aunt Penniman in *Washington Square*, she emphasises the free spirit's isolation; she reflects the muffling of these obscure tragedies by an uncomprehending society. Much of Newman's heroism lies in the lack of publicity which he gives his renunciation; much of his tragedy lies in his consequent loneliness and in the unshared burden of his grief. The lack of triumph and climax in the novel reflects the nature of this Jamesian heroism. James writes of Newman in his Preface to the novel: 'stricken, smarting, sore, he would arrive at his just vindication and then would fail of all triumphantly and all vulgarly enjoying it' (p. vii). As in *Washington Square* and *The Spoils of Poynton*, where the heroines similarly accept total forfeiture when their values are neglected by those around them, the hero is vindicated rather than triumphant. And just as Newman is unable to achieve any kind of resolution between freedom and form, between his needs and his environment, so the novel itself is less resolved in its conclusion than the later tragedies, and ends in a lower key. In these shorter works it is left to one final event to emphasise that the episode is closed. Newman's visit to the nunnery, Maurice Townsend's return, and the fire at Poynton establish that the interlude of hope and visions is over: life must go on as if such hope had never been.

The emphasis, therefore, is on continuity rather than finality. Life takes up where it left off, rather than being brought to a climax, or to a turning-point. The only change to be wrought by the upheaval is a reduction of expectations, a deadening of sensibility under the weight of loss. Newman's suffering is more in key with the disappointment of Catherine Sloper than with the anguish of Isabel Archer. He seems to share Catherine's feeling that 'nothing could ever undo the wrong or cure the pain' inflicted on each of them, but also her belief that, if there is something dead in one's life, his 'duty was to try and fill the void' (p. 215). Newman plans to fill the void by 'carrying out his life as he would have directed it had Mme de Cintré been left to him' (p. 462). But this purpose lacks any sense of development, any stake in the future, like the tending of a loved one's grave.

In the later tragedies, and to a lesser extent in *Roderick Hudson*, the sense of continuity is balanced by the finality of death; in *The American*, *Washington Square* and *The Spoils of Poynton*, the image of death-in-life stands alone. Because they lack the shaping conclusion characteristic of tragedy as a dramatic form, these works would be called 'tragic novels' or novellas, as distinct from tragedies. In spite of their exploration of the tragic themes which dominate James's fiction, they show that fidelity to life's inconclusiveness which is characteristic of the novel, rather than any tendency towards the structure of tragic drama. James here presents a conclusion that is no reaction of the moment, but one that must be lived with and sustained. For grand gestures rarely alter facts or affect consequences. It could be said that, in their subdued approach, these works are more faithful to the nature of their tragic subject than are the major tragedies. They illustrate what James, in his short story *Europe*, describes as 'that obscure, or at least that muffled, tragedy'[12] in a manner that breaks through that obscurity as little and as tactfully as possible.

(iii) 'THE PORTRAIT OF A LADY'

'You wanted to look at life for yourself – but you were not allowed; you were punished for your wish. You were ground in the very mill of the conventional.'[13] This is the way the dying Ralph Touchett summarises the tragedy of his cousin, Isabel Archer. Her tragedy, like Newman's, lies in the conflict between form and freedom, but the conflict is not simply between Isabel's desire for freedom, and the forms and restrictions imposed by the outside world. There is also an inner conflict between this desire and a yearning for form which lies in the very nature of Isabel's concept of freedom. The antithesis between form and freedom is neither simple nor constant. Ambiguity pervades these concepts as it does the cluster of ideas attaching to them. Through this haze of ambiguities Isabel has to define herself. This world of shifting appearances and meanings adds to her confusion, aiding and abetting her choice of a form of life which increasingly circumscribes her freedom. But Isabel has to come to terms with the forms of this world, seeking out that form which is appropriate to the free spirit.

Isabel's fondness for her liberty is almost the first, and certainly the most important characteristic of which the reader is made aware. Her independence of judgement is her pride. An orphan and so free of family ties, she is also, through her inheritance, to gain financial independence. She is determined to choose her own fate, believing she can thereby avoid suffering. But when she chooses Gilbert Osmond, her freedom is quickly and dramatically proved to be an illusion. Her wide aims are pathetically whittled down. Ralph's belief that Isabel is 'as good as her best opportunities' (I, 232), ironically provides the key to her fall. For the corrollary is that she may become as bad as her worst. Henrietta Stackpole, the journalist, seeing the effect of Gardencourt, the English home of the Touchetts, upon her friend, charges Isabel with a too ready adaptability. Isabel's very independence makes her especially vulnerable to change. Lacking any living tradition to impose or even suggest a particular style of life, lacking even a home, Isabel is prone to fit into any shape the occasion demands. However much she rebels against her aunt, Mrs Touchett's proprieties, she is easily absorbed into the idyllic and picturesque lifestyle of Gardencourt. Independent of people, Isabel is all the more dependent on circumstance.

Nowhere is the attraction of social forms for Isabel more evident than in the impact made upon her by the Old World. Europe is seen to stand for form, America for freedom. But, unlike Henrietta, who consistently acts out the role of the emancipated American female, Isabel loves Europe. In accepting Gilbert Osmond's proposal, she accepts a man who has rejected his native America for the older civilisation of Italy. Madame Merle, Mrs Touchett's somewhat mysterious friend, suggests that Isabel, with her 'actuality', belongs to the New World. But Isabel repeatedly rejects America in the person of Caspar Goodwood, the suitor who follows her from her Albany home. Caspar is reminiscent of Christopher Newman. He is so business-like and energetic that he seems 'to deprive her of the sense of freedom' (I, 142). The sense of life is so strong within him that it diminishes her own. His character is 'deficient in the social drapery commonly muffling . . .the sharpness of human contacts' (II, 246). Goodwood has little sense of social form. In contrast, the English landowner Lord Warburton has manners that are a guarantee he will cause no unpleasant scenes, whatever his feelings. But he too is rejected. In spite of her liking for the man, Isabel feels that 'a territorial, a political, a social magnate had conceived the design of drawing her into the system in which he rather invidiously lived and moved' (I, 127). He poses the same threat as Caspar. Osmond alone satisfies Isabel's requirements. His life is apparently dedicated to the forms of art, and his personal sense of form is such that he makes no threat to impinge upon her emotionally, declaring himself 'in a tone of almost impersonal discretion' (II, 16). The lover's excitement only reveals itself as 'a kind of ecstacy of self-control' (II, 68). He has the air of a man so self-contained that he can present no possible threat to another ego.

Isabel's freedom is, therefore, proved to be an illusion. She finds that Mme Merle, her husband's mistress, had planned Isabel's marriage to Osmond as a means to improving his fortunes. And Isabel's very concept of freedom is ambiguous. Her love of freedom is allied to her fear of involvement and personal commitment. She wishes to give, but not to be taken, to give her assets rather than herself. Fearing the physical and emotional disturbance which Caspar produces in her, she yet believes that, 'if a certain light should dawn she could give herself completely'. But this too she fears. For once Henrietta is to be taken seriously when she maintains that Isabel is a romantic, completely out of touch 'with the toiling, striving, suffering. . .sinning world' (I, 273); to make any success of life, Isabel must put her soul into it, for only then will life become a reality to her. The accusation is borne out by the symbolic bolted door of Isabel's childhood: 'she had no wish to look out, for this would have interfered with her theory that there was a strange, unseen place on the other side – a place which became to the child's imagination, according to its different moods, a region of delight or of terror' (I, 27).

The young woman keeps life at a distance by adopting the role of observer. References to observation and to ways of seeing are prolific. James mentions the 'comprehensiveness of observation' (I, 18) with which Isabel immediately takes in the scene at Gardencourt. He does not minimise the importance of observation. His characters are assessed in terms of their capacity for intelligent vision. In his personal writings he claims that 'when one should cease to live in large measure by one's eyes. . .one would have taken the longest step towards not living at all'.[14] But he also makes the reader aware of the limitations of vision. Isabel's position is illuminated by the presence of other 'observers' – Henrietta, for whom observation is a profession, and Ralph, whose role as spectator is forced upon him by ill-health. Ralph is painfully aware that he is deprived of any real involvement with life and with people, in particular with Isabel: 'Living as he now lived was like reading a good book in a poor translation' (I, 46). The reader may remember that Isabel, according to her brother-in-law, 'is written in a foreign tongue' (I, 34). Even Henrietta marries, apparently with success. Isabel admits that she does not wish 'to touch the cup of experience. It's a poisoned drink' (I, 188). She only wishes to see for herself. But although she claims that seeing and feeling are not incompatible, she distances experience until her feelings are of the order of theories. Her 'fine theory' (II, 65) about Gilbert Osmond misleads her totally about him. Seeing without involvement, she sees without moral judgement.

Isabel's ideal is incarnate in Mme Merle – 'a woman of strong impulses kept in admirable order' (I, 220). Her love of control – of controlled emotion and of controlled nature – is evident in her delight in visual order and in the picturesque. But by trying to see life in terms of picture and order, Isabel is opting for art rather than for life itself. The attraction Osmond has for her, in spite of being the antithesis of her confused urge to freedom, becomes more comprehensible against this background. She fails to realise that the man she envisages as her fellow-observer will inevitably regard her as an object, making her the observed of all observers. He will attempt to mould her into a work of art as he has done with his daughter Pansy, so like 'an Infanta of Velasquez' (II, 94).

For there is a difference not only in degree, but in kind between the two seekers after art and form. After Isabel's marriage, Pansy tells her friend Ed Rosier that, while her father still loves the visual and plastic arts, his new wife cares more for literature and conversation. When Isabel comes to Gardencourt, she sees it in literary as well as visual terms, Lord Warburton's presence making it 'just like a novel' (I, 16). 'The foundation of her knowledge' (I, 9) comes from books. Life is constantly intruding upon her literary experiences. But Isabel's literary leanings, like her role as observer, help her to keep life at a distance: she desires the disagreeable to enter her life because 'she had gathered from her acquaintance with literature that it was often a source of interest, and even of instruction' (I, 37). And yet, although literature may become a form of escapism, Isabel makes the reader aware of literature as a force which releases the imagination, which opens up new ideas and avenues of thought. In contrast, the plastic arts which Osmond admires can be seen as primarily a controlling power, forcing ideas into shape. Rather than releasing ideas in him, they already contain all that he desires, symbolising his materialistic worldliness. As a collector, he wants 'to keep, but not to add' (II, 91). The beautiful home in which Isabel lives as his wife grows to seem more and more claustrophobic and prison-like to her, while even Ralph's brief presence in Rome immediately makes her life seem 'more spacious' (II, 178), in the light of her cousin's unlimited generosity.

Furthermore, while Isabel is tempted to see life in terms of art, Osmond wishes to turn life into art. While Isabel seeks to channel her freedom into some meaningful form, Osmond wishes to replace freedom by form. The value of form for Osmond is like the pleasure of his Thursday evenings, held 'for the sake not so much of inviting people as of not inviting them'. (II, 257). Believing he loves convention as a symbol of harmony, order and decency, Isabel finds he loves it for its own sake. She felt 'the

aristocratic life was simply the union of great knowledge with
great liberty. . . But for Osmond it was altogether a thing of forms'
(II, 174). She mistakes his indifference for detachment, his inhumanity for objectivity. The sterility of his way of life is conveyed in James's summing up: Osmond's 'acquired habit. . .was
not that of succeeding, but it was something almost as good –
that of not attempting' (II, 236). Her ambitions end in 'a dark
narrow alley with a dead wall at the end' (II, 166). That ideal of
completeness which Isabel saw in Mme Merle is seen to be
emptiness, the death of the soul. And it is this that threatens
Isabel. 'The free, keen girl' is transformed into 'the fine lady who
was supposed to represent something' (II, 126) – that something
being Gilbert Osmond. In a carefully chosen image, Osmond
reveals all that he and Isabel respectively stand for: 'We're as
united, you know, as the candlestick and the snuffers' (II, 271).

If freedom is not to be found in detachment, then it appears
that freedom in its purest sense is not to be found at all. This is
the recognition Isabel must come to. In Richard Poirier's words,
'the longing for freedom ultimately becomes, the world being
what it is, the desire for death, for the "freedom and rest" which
James envied in Minny Temple'. But Poirier goes on to point
out that 'life finally denies Isabel [this] "freedom and rest". . .
the "eternal freedom" which is given to Minny and Ralph'.[15]
All that is possible in life is a limited kind of freedom. Ironically,
this is to be found in coming to terms with form – that is, with
the appropriate form, through commitment. Isabel finds it in her
marriage. She returns to Osmond not in conformity to his idea of
form, not with the idea of observing the proprieties of marriage,
but in adherence to her own ideal: 'one must accept one's deeds'
(II, 250). Isabel is determined not to repudiate 'the most serious
act – the single sacred act – of her life' (II, 216). She returns because she needs to keep faith not with Osmond, but with herself.
She fears the violence which would be done to her own integrity
by rejecting the destiny she chose for herself. Her marriage-vow
seems meaningless in the light of the trap which lured her into

that relationship. But Isabel can make it meaningful by adhering
to that vow by a truly free choice, based on reality.

In rejecting the example set by Mrs Touchett, estranged from
her husband and son, Isabel rejects the kind of freedom which
dries up the soul. She refuses to become 'an old woman without
memories' (II, 355). Unhappy memories are preferable to none.
And Isabel is sustained by a fluctuating conviction that she will
one day be happy again – 'it couldn't be she was to live only to
suffer. . .she was too valuable, too capable for that. . .She should
never escape; she should last to the end' (II, 343). Returning
may mean the end of her youthful dreams, but it is the only way
to freedom, through self-fulfilment.

The appropriateness of the form to which Isabel finally commits herself is evident in the relationship between the novel's end
and beginning. Her decision is a means of coming to terms with
Caspar, and her original rejection of him. When she leaves
America, he is 'the stubbornest fact' (I, 143) she knows, and she
is already aware that she will one day have to come to terms with
him. His strong masculinity tempts her to submission. She fears
that the happiness and security she would derive from marrying
him would cut her off from the unhappiness which is the fate
of the mass of men. This fate is also rightfully hers. It is the fate
of all who attempt to understand themselves and the nature of the
universe. Caspar offers the temptations of 'a clear and quiet harbour enclosed by a brave granite breakwater' (I, 284). His love
is, in its way, as great a threat to her freedom as Osmond's. Feeling his arms closing about her, and her own rapturous surrender,
Isabel understands the nature of this temptation. The harbour
which shelters also excludes. 'There was a very straight path'
(II, 381) – back to Osmond and her destiny as a suffering, think-
ing and feeling human being. 'She was free' (II, 381), but she
has paid a great price.

Isabel's search for an appropriate form is shared by her creator.
The thematic tension between form and freedom is reflected in an
aesthetic tension. *The Portrait of a Lady* is the most striking and

successful example of the balance between tragedy and the novel characteristic of many of James's novels. The desire for a restraining, shaping force in life suggests the classical ideal of order and restraint in art. In this novel the traditional form and pattern of tragedy holds in check the tendency of the realistic narrative towards expansiveness and the breaking of bounds. The title of the novel suggests a framing of experience, a sense of completion which recalls the unity of classical tragedy, although the reader remains constantly aware of life's resistance to form, of life forcing itself through any arbitrary attempt to define ends and beginnings.

This formal tension is evident in James's use of dialogue and narration. He alternates the spoken word – thought given verbal form – and the unspoken idea, the free flow of an individual's thoughts and feelings as conveyed through the narrative. The passages of narrative give the spoken word a wealth of unspoken meaning. There are degrees of formality in speech, of course. There is a distinction between conversational 'small talk', an integral tool in the preservation of social form, and language as real communication. James accentuates this distinction by contrasting American frankness and European reticence. Old Mr Touchett has still not learnt what, for the English, is not said. The Old World respect for reticence and propriety prevents feelings from being directly expressed. The demands of form interfere with freedom of speech. The publicity to which Isabel is exposed in her role as a leading figure in fashionable Italian society makes her constantly aware of the dangers of betraying her feelings. Suppressed, they are intensified. Ralph sees a 'kind of violence in some of her impulses' (II, 125): the strength of her pent-up emotions continually seeks release in some form. Such realities are not to be found in the kind of social intercourse which Osmond and Mme Merle maintain so well that it strikes Isabel as having 'the rich readiness that would have come from rehearsal' (I, 313). They are to be found in more intimate moments. Revelation frequently comes in silence. As suspicion is cast on the validity of language as a form of expression, so meaning is sought and found elsewhere. Isabel learns everything about her husband's relationship with Mme Merle when she disturbs the two alone in silence — he sitting, she standing, the forms reversed.

The threat of disruption and violence increases with the demands of restraint, of life lived as art. When the truth is uttered, the effect is emphasised by its rarity. Much of the impact Caspar Goodwood makes both on Isabel and on the reader is due to his refusal to respect the proprieties. He frequently leaves her weeping with exhausted emotion, telling her, for instance, that he would rather think of her as dead than as married to another man. And when Isabel and Osmond speak alone together, the cool deliberation with which he delivers his bitterness starkly conveys that these are not reactions engendered by the heat of the moment. The interaction of scene and narrative reiterates the suggestion that the tragic experience is all one and continuous. It is not confined to dramatic moments of crisis which bring the feelings of anger and suffering to the surface. Frequently it does not surface to the public gaze at all, but continues behind the scenes. The tragedy is not 'the scene of a moment; it will be a scene that will last always' (II, 348).

James frequently glosses over the potentially most dramatic events and crises. What might seem to be the novel's turning-point — Isabel's acceptance of and marriage to Osmond — is narrated, not dramatised, and the death of her only child is hardly touched on. What matters is not the isolated event, but its consequences, its everyday reality and apparently minor, but cumulative, frustrations. The death of Isabel's child is only one of the several factors causing the great emptiness in her life, which is the major 'event'. In spite of the confusion of crisis and consequence a traditional tragic pattern is evident. The quest for self-knowledge and fulfilment reveals itself to be a characteristically cyclical journey. The cyclical, repetitive elements of tragedy are evident even to Isabel when she recalls that Osmond's words to her outside St Peter's in Rome — 'I didn't come for the others' (I, 376) — are the same as those spoken to her by Lord Warburton on the day he proposed. This time, however, she fails to recognise the threat. On returning to Gardencourt she is again aware of life repeating itself, but this time it is Caspar in Lord Warburton's place, and this time she has learned enough to resist. The end takes us back to the beginning, the cycle is complete, the journey of discovery is over. But although this traditional pattern provides an outline for the novel's structure, it is given a characteristically modern treatment. The chronological progress of the tragedy is constantly halted to provide the kind of detail and social background of a character's experience that belong to the novel as a genre. The mere action is complemented by the innumerable factors and conditions which give each situation its particular essence. The complexity and variety of life resist the formal pattern, suggesting that cause and effect cannot be neatly allocated, but are inextricably intertwined, as is the individual's free will with the realities around him.

As we cannot say where cause begins and effect ends, so we cannot strictly say that Isabel's journey is over. The story of *The Portrait of a Lady* may be complete, but not the story of Isabel Osmond. The novel's ending maintains a careful balance between formal finality and a realistic sense of continuity. James himself comments on the careful shaping of the novel: its ' "architectural" competence' makes it 'the most proportioned' of all his productions, apart from *The Ambassadors* (preface p. xviii). He writes, 'What I have done has that unity – it groups together. It is complete in itself – and the rest may be taken up or not, later'.[16] He is not suggesting that he may finish the story, but that the reader may. The tragic pattern is complete when Isabel comes to terms with her destiny. In her return to Italy there is something of the traditional idea of spiritual triumph through death. Her renunciation of her physical freedom, her abnegation of her own desires, constitutes a kind of death of the flesh through which her soul triumphs. In aesthetic terms this is both climax and end. But James also means the reader to feel that Isabel has now to live out her decision, so that the idea of continuity persists. It is emphasised by comparison with the traditional 'closed' endings of marriage and death which tie up the fates of Henrietta and Ralph. Tragedy and the novel, form and freedom, are held in balance, each heightening the power of the other. Isabel's fear of the violent and emotional undercurrents in life and in herself, of raw, chaotic experience bursting through the veneer of civilisation, is mirrored in the novel's form. The shapelessness of directly recorded experience and its endless ramifications constantly threatens to disrupt the neoclassical tragic superstructure James has created. Such an achieved tension is one of James's major aims. He believes the novel as a genre has power 'to appear more true to its character in proportion as it strains, or tends to burst, with a latent extravagance, its mould'. (*The Ambassadors*, preface p. xi.)

(iv) 'THE WINGS OF THE DOVE': THE ESSENCE OF TRAGEDY?

James described the image of his cousin Minnie Temple, clinging to consciousness in the face of death, as 'of the essence of tragedy . . .Death, at the last, was dreadful to her; she would have given anything to live'. This image was so intense that he was 'in the far-off aftertime to seek to lay the ghost by wrapping it, a particular occasion aiding, in the beauty and dignity of art'.[17] The result was *The Wings of the Dove*. In focusing the novel on Milly Theale's death, James is aware of following the dominant tragic tradition, 'as if to be menaced with death or danger hadn't been from time immemorial, for heroine or hero, the very shortest of all cuts to the interesting state'.[18] But this does not constitute such a radical departure from his conception of tragedy as more a matter of life, than of death, than it might at first seem.

Milly's possible death is increasingly the most important fact about her. Together with her immense wealth, it provides both the cause and the pathos of her betrayal. Isabel Archer is genuinely desired as a wife as well as an heiress; Milly, rich as she is, is only seriously sought in marriage when the extent of her illness becomes known. Her fatality is her great value: '*she* mightn't last, but her money would' (II, 135). The pathos of her situation ironically further isolates her. The experience of dying is inaccessible to the healthy. And sympathy itself increases her loneliness, for it is a substitute for a genuine response to Milly as an individual. The sympathy is for her situation, not an attempt to identify with her personality. Her identity is submerged in an image, in the 'princess' or 'the American girl'. No one really sees her. Densher significantly thinks of her as 'little', although she is as tall as Kate. Sympathy precludes real relationships. Milly is intensely disappointed that Densher shares '*the* view', because it 'anticipated and superseded the – likewise sweet – operation of real affinities' (I, 265). This view is symptomatic of the tendency to see Milly as an object, as a curiosity, to be used and to be pitied.

The state of isolated passivity to which Milly's doom reduces her is surely one of the consequences James had in mind when he expressed the need 'so closely to cross-question that idea of making one's protagonist sick'. He doubted whether the hero should meet his death in such a way that his whole life, as the reader sees it, is itself the act of dying. But, whatever other fields of activity are closed to such a protagonist, there remains the 'unsurpassable activity of passionate, of inspired resistance' (preface, p. vii). Susan Shepherd soon realises that 'the future wasn't to exist for her princess in the form of any sharp or simple release from the human predicament. . .It would be a question of taking full in the face the whole assault of life' (I, 112). Tragedy is never ultimately concerned with death. It is the light which imminent and inevitable death throws on the nature of life which is important:

the poet essentially *can't* be concerned with the act of dying. Let him deal with the sickest of the sick, it is still by the act of living that they appeal to him, and appeal the more as the conditions plot against them and prescribe the battle. The process of life gives way fighting, and often may so shine out on the lost ground as in no other connexion (preface, p. vii).

The illumination is strongest for the doomed. Milly intuitively grasps the value of living each day as if it were the last, even before she is fully aware of the relevance of such a philosophy to herself. The feeling that time is running out imparts an urgency and value to each choice, because she is now shaping her destiny once and for all. The chance will not be repeated. In contrast, Kate Croy and Densher feel that time is on their side, and constantly postpone their life together, so that they finally lose their chance of happiness. Milly's understanding and appreciation of every experience is heightened by her situation. Her visit to the beautiful country house, Matcham, becomes 'a sort of magnificent maximum, the pink dawn of an apotheosis' (I, 195). The Bronzino portrait, so like herself, reinforces her and the reader's impression that this is 'perhaps as good a moment as she should have with any one, or have in any connexion whatever' (I, 195). This is the peak at which Milly too will, as it were, be immortalised. She has a complete, throbbing awareness of how it feels to be alive. She has wealth, youth, goodness and beauty, and is to lose it all. The loss not only of all this, but of all she might have had, is the agonising prospect before her. The meaning of death is all the clearer in the light of all she has learned of the meaning of life. She dies, but more important, she dies cheated, made aware of life only to lose it. It is not the end of life, but the end of its real beginning, that is tragic.

Milly is, moreover, in a position to question the values of others, to judge of their ultimate importance. Freed both by her illness and by her wealth from trivial practical concerns, she perhaps can judge what man is to live by if he cannot live by bread alone. And yet European society seems based on the assumption that he can. Everything is seen in financial terms, in terms of its exchange value. Kate claims to value money as a means to freedom, which it seems to be for Milly. But even she suspects that 'Mildred Theale was not, after all, a person to change places, to change even chances with' (I, 156). Milly is free of family, as of financial pressures, yet hers is 'a caged freedom' (II, 150). Her

freedom is due more to her illness than to her money: she is
allowed to move freely only because the bars of her cage are so
immovable. Money is also desired as a means to cultural values,
to things of beauty. But it simply takes Kate from the vulgarity
of a mean home to her aunt, Mrs Lowder, and the vulgarity of
display. The confusion of values is reflected in the confusion of
terms: 'the great ugliness' (1, 56) is poverty; Kate's beauty, on
the other hand, is 'a tangible value' (1, 8). Densher and Milly's
loyal friend, Susan Shepherd, the representatives of the world of
the minds, the writers, are significantly those with least wealth
and show. In so money-conscious a society, the usual moral
values are distorted. Densher's only answer to Lancaster Gate is
'that he loved the girl – which in such a house as that was painfully cheap' (1, 70). Love and family loyalty are dismissed as of no
importance. Individuals still cling to some kind of personal
standard, but their morality becomes bizarre and distorted under
so many pressures. Densher betrays Milly out of loyalty to Kate;
Lord Mark insists on telling Milly the truth about Kate and
Densher – a truth that kills. All values are relative. Even Susan,
'the woman in the world least formed by nature. . .for duplicities
and labyrinths' (1, 94), finds herself involved in subtlety and
calculation. The cause is her new relationship with Milly. The one
stable value in the fact of death is kindness. However mixed
their motives, all the characters feel this to be the only response
to Milly, the only thing of unquestionable value. When the
touchstone of her fatality is applied, only loving-kindness remains.

But a greater insight into the nature of life and its values can
be gained by considering what it is that sustains life, the absence
of which kills. In a literal sense, it is Milly's illness that kills her.
But Milly decides to die when she turns her face to the wall. This
suggests that there is something more fundamental at issue than
health. Kate recognises, after Milly's death, that Milly 'was living
by will. . .then her will, at a given moment, broke down' (11,
286). Susan Shepherd describes how much Milly wanted to live,

in terms that remind the reader of James's description of his cousin. There is a subtle distinction between wanting to live and having the will to live. Milly wants to live, but lacks the will. That is, she lacks the guarantees of happiness necessary to give her the immense will required to stretch out her life to its utmost. She does not want to live to no purpose. What truly separates life from death is this volition that grows from the possession of something – or more often someone – that makes life worth living.

This will to live also requires a great act of faith. Although acceptance of death is the only means to living fully, Milly must live 'as if' – as if life were all, and death were nothing. Knowing death, she must yet believe in life; knowing evil, she must yet believe in good. An undercurrent of violence, generated largely by the threats to Milly's life and happiness, permeates the novel. The novel's imagery suggests that the social system is based upon the law of the jungle: Kate is likened to a 'panther' (I, 248), and at Lancaster Gate Densher is 'in the cage of the lioness without his whip' (I, 70). But only an outsider like Susan sees, in the English circle's treatment of Milly, 'the oddity of a Christian maiden, in the arena, mildly, caressingly, martyred' (II, 38). The treachery is concealed beneath a civilised, even loving exterior. Milly herself only knows the threat concealed within her own body. But in Kate's company, even she sometimes feels completely 'taken up with the unspoken. . .conscious of being here on the edge of a great darkness' (I, 168). For Milly, the unspoken remains the unknown; for Kate and Densher, the known must remain unspoken. This horror binds them together in 'the need to bury in the dark blindness of each other's arms the knowledge of each other that they couldn't undo' (II, 347). Yet Milly seems to sanction this universal deceit. She shares the universal desire for silence with regard to her illness and her delicate relationship with Densher. To be explicit would be to 'bring down the avalanche' (II, 127). To acknowledge the violence beneath the surface is to give in to chaos. When Milly learns the truth, Densher sees it is the obliteration of 'the margin on a faith in which they were all living' (II, 233-4).

But Milly's act of faith differs from the general creed because it includes what is totally lacking in theirs – imagination. She not only denies reality, but offers an alternative. 'The dove' is able to rise above the system, while the others remain enmeshed in it. Kate's imagination can only stretch to visualising alternatives within the existing structure. By substituting for give and take the principle of giving, Milly is freed from personal involvement, yet totally committed to life. In her predicament, she has no time for bargains and agreements, knowing how little guarantee she can give of fulfilling her part. She commits herself without condition, clause or codicil, holding nothing back for the future because the future is all too certain. If Milly dies cheated, it is nonetheless true that Milly cheats death. It can take nothing from her that she herself has not already given.

Milly's death may have been inspired by the author's personal experience, but its value in fictional terms lies in its symbolic function. The universality of death and its critical nature shows simultaneously the common nature of man and the distinctive qualities of the individual man. Death highlights the fate that unites at the moment that most isolates. James's reiteration of the dove symbol, as of the princess imagery associated with it, reinforces the generalising power of this central experience. Milly herself makes the connection as she mixes with the inhabitants of London:

Their box, their great common anxiety, what was it, in this grim breathing-space, but the practical question of life? They could live if they would; that is, like herself, they had been told so: she saw them all about her, on seats, digesting the information, recognising it again as something in a slightly different shape familiar enough, the blessed old truth that they would live if they could. (I, 221)

James is not talking here simply in terms of life and death, but in terms of quality of life – of the life that is worth living and the life that is not. Milly's death symbolises both the death that comes to all and that 'death-in-life' that is James's distinctive conception of the tragic fate.

To suggest this relationship between death and death-in-life, James uses Kate as a point of comparison with Milly. Her situation is in many ways similar. Like Milly and Susan, she and Densher form a pair of opposites. Densher represents the mind for Kate, just as Susan represents culture for Milly. On arrival at Lancaster Gate, Kate fears 'going down' from her refuge as much as Milly clings to the 'image of never going down', in her Venetian palace. Kate feels herself safe in 'the provisioned citadel' (I, 27), as Milly feels safe 'as in a fortress' (II, 133). Kate also wants to live, but in trying to do so at Milly's expense, she effectually ends both lives. The ending of her relationship with Densher makes a grim contrast with its beginning. Kate, too, has lost her one and only chance. Worse, like Mme Merle, she has lost her soul. Densher himself feels in some way blessed and sanctified by his experience. But he has to endure a loss 'which was like the sight of a priceless pearl cast before his eyes – his pledge given not to save it – into the fathomless sea, or rather even it was like the sacrifice of something sentient and throbbing, something that, for the spiritual ear, might have been audible as a faint far wail' (II, 351). He is aware that this sound will only remain 'till the inevitable sounds of life, once more, comparatively coarse and harsh, should smother and deaden it – doubtless by the same process with which they would officiously heal the ache in his soul that was somehow one with it' (II, 351), but this process of healing is itself regretted. It means the extinction of the most intensely felt, even if the most painful, phase of his life. In order to ensure that the reader is not, as he would otherwise tend to be, too involved in Milly's experience to be able to appreciate fully the predicament of the lovers – of those who must live with the consequences of her death – Milly's death is not dramatised, but reported. While using these two characters to present Milly's tragedy, James suggests the nature of their own, which is bound up with their meeting with a life which could not be assimilated by theirs. In this ending James combines the traditional tragic note with a concept of tragedy which is more characteristically his own.

The continuity of the idea of tragic death and the idea of tragic life is evident in the thematic and verbal links between *The Wings of the Dove* and *Roderick Hudson*. In the earlier novel, James describes the loss of Roderick's talent in words which anticipate his description of the loss of Milly's life. These are Roderick's reactions:

> Remember that hereafter. Don't say that he was stupefied and senseless; that his perception was dulled and his aspiration dead. Say that he trembled in every nerve with a sense of the beauty and sweetness of life: that he rebelled and protested and struggled; say he was buried alive, with his eyes open and his heart beating to madness; say he clung to every blade of grass and every wayside thorn as he passed; say it was the most pathetic thing you ever beheld. (p. 410)

Milly's reactions come to us through Susan: 'She doesn't WANT to die. Think of her age. Think of her goodness. Think of her beauty. Think of all she is. Think of all she *has*. She lies there stiffening herself and clinging to it all' (II, 245). Roderick clings to his life as Milly does. His feeling that his life will end with his talent is not fulfilled either with any great logic or to James's satisfaction, but its implications are clear enough. Roderick is now living only by habit; he has 'no will left' (p. 414). He wants to live again, but he lacks that which Rowland Mallett also seeks: 'something that might make one's tenure of life strong and zealous instead of mechanical and uncertain' (p. 274), the guarantee that Milly looks for. The loss of the ability to work is living death for Roderick because it involves the death of the faculties that give life meaning, that give sense and form to his imagination and make him aware of the life around him. His actual death adds little, if anything, to his tragedy. James's use of death in *The Wings of the Dove* is more central to the tragedy than it is in *Roderick Hudson*, but it does not constitute a real divergence from his usual conception of tragedy. *The Wings of the Dove* should be seen as a work in which James uses the irrevocable finality of death as the most emotionally powerful and immediate image of tragic loss. But this image should not blind the reader to those lingering 'deaths' which last a life-time. The essence of tragedy is not in the death but in the life – in the living consciousness of loss and waste. It is not death but life that James calls 'terrible, tragic, perverse and abysmal'.[19]

CONCLUSION

My Introduction showed that the Victorian tragic novelists were often praised as moral teachers and as creators of new, more relevant kinds of tragedy. But at other times they were condemned for their realism, for portraying characters and situations incapable of arousing the tragic response, in a genre which lacked the formal and aesthetic qualities which might compensate for the painfulness and ugliness depicted. The most constructive point to emerge from this debate was the suggestion that the novel's bias towards realism was not necessarily a limitation: instead it was possible that this bias might interact with the idealised formal principles of tragic drama in a way that would unite the contemporary and the universal, both essential in a living tragedy.

Novelists tackled the problems involved in the creation of a contemporary and more 'realistic' form of tragedy in different ways. They could redefine the concept of tragedy in terms more appropriate to the contemporary situation, or attempt to convey traditional tragic ideas through new subjects, such as the working class. In either case, the novelist had to prove the validity of his version of tragedy. Whether explicitly, through an omniscient narrator, or indirectly, through highly articulate and conscious characters, or through symbolism and imagery, each attempted to establish the connection between individuals in specific contemporary situations, and the universal human condition. But they simultaneously retained the sense of the specifically social which makes these tragic novels such significant representations of tragic suffering.

George Eliot's redefinition of tragedy resulted finally in an avoidance of tragedy, both as theme and form. In comparing her novels with Hardy's, it becomes clear that her rejection of the traditional tragic vision in favour of a more comprehensive vision is reflected in the form of her novels, which contains and qualifies the tragic elements: she exploited the novel as a genre which will not so much succeed tragic drama, as put it into perspective.

Hardy's novels show a preoccupation with tragic themes which developed in his later work into something that might be called tragedy, rather than merely tragic, something that reflects in novelistic terms the idealised and poetic conventions of tragic drama. The form of his novels is dominated by the tragic elements, mirroring the exclusiveness of his tragic vision. Adopting the traditional concept of tragedy, he necessarily adopted the traditional patterns and structures evolved to express that concept. At the same time, like George Eliot, he was aware of the need for modern images of tragedy and this search eventually demanded a correspondingly modern, rather than ancient, form.

In Henry James's novels the influence of tragedy is less easy to pin-point. Many of his novels centre on tragic themes, both traditional and Jamesian, but few can be called tragedies – that is, few focus exclusively on the tragic situation, or use the novel's structure to isolate and highlight the tragic pattern. Even in the exceptions, the traditional tragic model never dominates the novel as it does Hardy's; it is balanced by those characteristics of the realistic novel which best express the contrasting modern concept of tragedy. His tragic novels provide the most striking instance of the relationship between theme and form. In his work the tension between genres, between tragedy and the novel – what I have called form and freedom – reflects the tragic conflict, the novel's theme.

As far as a general conclusion is either possible or desirable, I would suggest that there is a necessary relationship between tragic theme and tragic form: the more closely the novelist adheres to traditional tragic themes and concepts, the more his work is shaped by the formal characteristics of tragic drama, rather than by the novel's originally realistic bias.

But the influence of tragic themes and forms on the novel is not, of course, limited to the Victorian period. Such influences are evident both before and after. There is a natural continuity between the novelists under discussion and their immediate successors. Joseph Conrad's novels show the same preoccupation with the individual's inability to escape his past; it reveals itself, for instance, in his concentration on memory and remorse in *Lord Jim* (1900). In Jack London's *Martin Eden* we have what could be called an American *Jude the Obscure*, while Hardy's pessimistic exploration of sexual relationships is continued more notably by D.H. Lawrence. Frank Kermode, however, links Lawrence with George Eliot: he refers to the scene in which 'Lawrence allows Gudrun to think of herself as a modern Hetty Sorrel, and of Gerald as a modern Arthur Donnithorne. It is a thought full of irony and the recognition of a change in the patterns of sexual tragedy'.[1] For C.B. Cox the tragic predicament of the 'free spirit' in society unites the work of George Eliot and Henry James with that of E.M. Forster in this century.[2] This is not the place for an extended discussion of the place of tragedy in the twentieth-century novel, but novelists have clearly continued to concern themselves with tragic experience, and to face the kind of problems that the concept of 'realistic' tragedy posed for the Victorian novelists.

For it remains true that tragedy in art is and must be quite different from tragedy in life. Tragedy in life cannot be rendered in terms of art, as C.S. Lewis points out:

For unfortunately the play is not over. We have no EXEUNT OMNES. The real story does not end: it proceeds to ringing up undertakers, paying bills, getting death certificates. . .There is no grandeur and no finality. . .The tragedian dare not present the totality of suffering as it usually is in its uncouth mixture of agony with littleness, all the indignities and (save for the pity) the uninterestingness of grief. It would ruin his play. It would be merely dull and depressing. He selects from reality just what his art needs; and what it needs is the exceptional.

(*Experiment in Criticism*, 1961, p. 78.)

A novelist like George Eliot may attempt to give a more realistic rendering of tragic experience as it occurs in life, continuing the story beyond the point at which the tragedian would end. The novel can perhaps bring to the portrayal of tragedy a degree of realism beyond the scope of the dramatist. But our very use of the term 'realism' acknowledges that realism is not reality, but merely another convention for the representation of reality. In suggesting that a more contemporary convention can be found to convey to a modern public the illusion of tragic experience, we may simply be avoiding the central issue. For the modern concept of tragedy – that is, of the tragic experience – is essentially anti-formal and anti-literary. It is no longer a question of reconciling two literary modes – realism and traditional tragedy – but of finding any valid form of literary expression for a vision of reality which is the antithesis of art and order. Realistic tragedy becomes a contradiction in terms not because of the limitations of realism, but because tragedy itself seems an increasingly suspect literary form.. It is suspect because it purports to create beauty out of horror, to make 'all disagreeables evaporate, from their being in close relationship with Beauty and Truth',[3] thereby falsifying the experience it sets out to convey. In his book *The Tragic Vision*, Murray Krieger attempts to clarify this issue by distinguishing between tragedy as an art-form and the tragic vision which developed within that form but has since burst beyond its limits. As the pessimism and chaos of that vision increased, it could no longer be contained by that aesthetic form which, in its sense of order, contradicts this darkness: 'so long as tragedy remained a defined literary form, the fearsome chaotic necessities of the tragic vision would have to surrender finally to the higher unity which contained them', seeming to guarantee 'cosmic. order'.[4] The novel, as a less defined literary form may again seem to offer itself as a more satisfactory vehicle for such a vision. Doubts about the validity of traditional tragic form are prefigured in Hardy's development: whereas his tragic vision can be said to be contained in the tragedy of *Tess of the D'Urbervilles*, in *Jude the Obscure* it is unrelieved, breaking through the style established by the earlier novels to create a quite different literary form, a form which perhaps heralds the treatment of tragedy in the twentieth-century novel. But we may have to go even further away from the traditional concept of tragedy than this.

For one of the most important attempts to convey the contemporary tragic vision in a form which will not contradict its pessimism and chaos can be found in *The Theatre of the Absurd*. This 'strives to express its sense of the senselessness of the human condition and the inadequacy of the rational approach by the open abandonment of rational devices and discursive thought. . .trying to achieve a unity between its basic assumptions and the form in which these are expressed'.[5] This group of dramatists has abandoned not only the formal concept of tragedy, but the very category of the tragic, adopting an inclusive category which supersedes those of tragedy and comedy for many representative moderns. Martin Esslin attempts to explain this reconciliation of the comic and tragic by reference to the manner of characterisation typical of the Absurd: 'As the incomprehensibility of the motives, and the often unexplained and mysterious nature of the characters' actions. . .effectively prevent identification, such theatre is a comic theatre in spite of the fact that its subject-matter is sombre, violent and bitter.'[6] The modern playwright, it appears, deliberately excludes that sympathy which the nineteenth-century critics assumed to be essential to tragedy. The attempt to achieve a more truthful match between tragic experience and tragic form – an attempt which we have seen as a driving force among the Victorian tragic novelists – has apparently led to the abandonment of tragedy not simply as a form but as a concept with its own unique identity and significance.

NOTES

INTRODUCTION: THE CRITICAL BACKGROUND

1 Anonymous review of *The Trials of Margaret Lyndsay*, *Blackwood's Edinburgh Magazine*, 13, 1823, p. 549.
2 *Essays by the Late George Brimley*, ed. by W.G. Clark, 1860, pp. 294–5.
3 *Views and Reviews*, 2 vols., 1890, I, p. 49.
4 *Aristotle's Theory of Poetry and Fine Art*, trans. S.H. Butcher, 4th edition, 1907, p. 53 and p. 45.
5 'The Two Tragedies – a note', *Blackwood's Edinburgh Magazine*, 162, 1897, p. 395.
6 Quoted by Raymond Williams, *The Long Revolution*, 1961, p. 276.
7 'The Novels of Jane Austen', *Blackwood's Edinburgh Magazine*, 86, 1859, p. 102.
8 L.J. Jennings, '*The Portrait of a Lady*', *Quarterly Review*, 155, 1883, p. 214.
9 'Preface to First Edition of Poems (1853)', *Irish Essays and Others*, 1904, p. 273.
10 'The Principles of Success in Literature', *Fortnightly Review*, 1, 1865, p. 589.
11 'Henry James's Achievements', *Edinburgh Review*, 197, 1903, p. 85.
12 Anonymous review of '*Daniel Deronda*', *Edinburgh Review*, 144, 1876, p. 446.
13 *Essays and Reviews*, Edinburgh, 1876, pp. 363–4.
14 *Views and Reviews*, I, p. 52.
15 'Recent Tragedies', *Westminster Review*, 37, 1842, p. 338.

Chapter 1. *The tragic philosophy: determinism and free will*

1 *Adam Bede*, 2 vols., I, p. 55. All quotations from George Eliot's novels are from the Cabinet edition of *The Works of George Eliot*, 20 vols., Edinburgh and London, 1878–80.
2 *Felix Holt, the Radical*, 2 vols., I, p. 72.
3 *Middlemarch: A Study of Provincial Life*, 3 vols., II, p. 289.

4 *The Wings of the Dove*, 2 vols., 1923, I, p. 30. All quotations from Henry James's novels are from the Macmillan edition of *The Novels and Stories of Henry James*, 35 vols., 1921–3. The text is that of the New York Edition, 1907–17.

5 *Ibid.*, I, p. 142.

6 *Ibid.*, I, p. 187.

7 *The Portrait of a Lady*, 2 vols., I, p. 241.

8 F.E. Hardy, *The Later Years of Thomas Hardy 1892–1928*, 1930, p. 27.

9 *Longman's Magazine*, 2, 1883, pp. 252–69.

10 Attributed to Hardy by Raymond Blathwayt, 'A Chat with the Author of *Tess*', *Black and White*, 27 August 1892, p. 238.

11 'The Waiting Supper', *A Changed Man, The Waiting Supper and Other Tales, Concluding with The Romantic Adventures of a Milkmaid*, 1913, p. 30. All quotations from Thomas Hardy's novels are from the Wessex Edition, 21 vols., 1912–13.

12 *Romola*, 2 vols., I, p. 340.

13 'The Noble School of Fiction', *Nation*, 6 July 1865, p. 22.

14 F.E. Hardy, *Later Years*, p. 8.

Chapter 2.   From tragic drama to the tragic novel

1 See Augustin Filon, *The English Stage: An Account of the Victorian Drama*, 1897, for a contemporary view, and Allardyce Nicoll, *A History of English Drama 1660–1900*, 6 vols., 1952–9, vols. IV and V, for a more recent perspective.

2 Review of *Sardanapalus, The Two Foscari* and *Cain, Blackwood's Magazine* II, 1822, p. 91.

3 *The English Stage*, p. 175 and p. 176.

4 *Views and Reviews*, I, p. 85.

5 cf. G.H. Lewes' comment, Introduction, p. 13.

6 *George Eliot: A Biography*, 1968, and *The George Eliot Letters*, 7 vols., 1954–5, have been invaluable sources for this chapter, as for any information about George Eliot's life and work.

7 *George Eliot Letters*, IV, p. 428.

8 Haight, *George Eliot*, p. 388.

9 '*Felix Holt* as Classic Tragedy', *Nineteenth Century Fiction* 16, 1961, p. 57.

10 *Aeschylus: The Creator of Tragedy*, ed. and trans. 1940, l. 160

11 *Henry James, The Untried Years 1843–1870*, 1953, p. 155 and pp. 215–16.

12 *The Letters of Henry James*, ed. by Percy Lubbock, 2 vols., 1920, II, p. 94.

13 'Henry James at the Grecian Urn', *PMLA*, 66, 1951, p. 317.

14 'The Profitable Reading of Fiction', *Forum*, 5, 1888, p. 69.
15 'The Natural History of German Life', *Westminster Review*, 66, 1856, p. 58 and p. 61.
16 *George Eliot Letters*, IV, p. 301.
17 'Amos Barton', *Scenes of Clerical Life*, 2 vols., I, p. 66.
18 *Romola*, 3 vols., II, p. 102.
19 *The Letters of W.B. Yeats*, edited by Allan Wade, 1954, p. 128.
20 *Thomas Hardy's Notebooks*, edited by Evelyn Hardy, 1955, p. 37.
21 See Chapter 6 of this study.
22 *The Notebooks of Henry James*, edited by F.O. Matthiesson and Kenneth B. Murdock, 1947, pp. 182–3.
23 Preface to *The Spoils of Poynton, A London Life, The Chaperon*, p. xvii.
24 *The Notebooks of Henry James*, p. 144.

Chapter 3. Realism and tragedy

1 *An Experiment in Criticism*, 1961, p. 59.
2 *The Long Revolution*, 1961, p. 287.
3 *Macbeth*, iv. 3. p. 219.
4 'The Dynasts', *Poetical Works of Thomas Hardy*, III, p. 109.
5 Preface to *The Ambassadors*, 2 vols., 1923, I, p. xxi.
6 E.g. the Lady-Day removal appears in *Tess*, pp. 449–50.
7 'General Preface to The Novels and Poems', *Tess of the D'Urbervilles*, p. ix.
8 *Westminster Review*, 66, 1856, pp. 51–79.
9 'The Future of German Philosophy', *Leader*, 28 July 1855, p. 723.
10 'The Critic as Artist', *The Artist as Critic: Critical Writings of Oscar Wilde*, edited by Richard Ellmann, 1970, p. 383.
11 *Later Years*, p. 16.
12 Preface to *Roderick Hudson*, p. xix.
13 *Phoenix: The Posthumous Papers of D.H. Lawrence*, edited by Edward Macdonald, 1936, p. 516.
14 *Tragedy is Not Enough*, 1953, p. 48.
15 *The Return of the Native*, pp. 78–9.

Chapter 4. George Eliot: pathos and tragedy

1 *New York Times*, 27 February 1947, sec. 2, p. 1.
2 'The Novels of George Eliot', *Atlantic Monthly*, 18, 1866, p. 487.
3 *Middlemarch*, II, p. 121 and II, p. 126.
4 *The Mill on the Floss*, I, pp. 407–8 and II, p. 64.
5 'The *Antigone* and its Moral', *Leader*, 29 March 1856, p. 306.

6 *The Mill on the Floss*, I, p. 382. All further references to this novel will follow the relevant quotations in the text.

7 *George Eliot Letters*, III, p. 318.

8 *Ibid.*, III, p. 374.

9 See p. 91.

10 Quoted by J.W. Cross, *George Eliot's Life as Related in her Letters and Journals*, 3 vols., 1885, III, p. 44 and III, p. 42.

11 *Ibid.*, III, p. 47.

12 *Ibid.*, III, p. 43.

13 *Ibid.*, III, p. 42.

14 *Ibid.*, III, p. 45.

15 *Henry James and H.G. Wells: A Record of their Friendship, Their Debate on the Art of Fiction and their Quarrel*, edited by Leon Edel and Gordon N. Ray, 1958, p. 152.

16 *Daniel Deronda*, III, 240 and III, 344–5.

17 '*Strafford* and the Historical Drama', *Westminster Review*, 41, 1844, p. 119.

18 'Evangelical Teaching: Dr Cumming', *Westminster Review*, 64, 1855, pp. 460–1.

19 'The Novels of George Eliot', *Atlantic Monthly*, 18, 1866, p. 485.

Chapter 5. Thomas Hardy: tragedy ancient and modern

1 'For Conscience Sake', *Life's Little Ironies*, 1912, pp. 73–4.

2 *Early Life*, p. 289.

3 *Later Years*, p. 14.

4 'The Profitable Reading of Fiction', *Forum*, 5, 1888, p. 67.

5 'The Profitable Reading of Fiction', p. 69.

6 'Why I don't write plays', *Pall Mall Gazette*, 31 August 1892, p. 1.

7 'Candour in English Fiction', *New Review*, 2, 1890, p. 16.

8 *The Return of the Native*, p. 77. All further references to this novel will follow the relevant quotations in the text.

9 See footnote, *The Return of the Native*, p. 473.

10 See, for example: D.A. Dike, 'A Modern Oedipus: *The Mayor of Casterbridge*', *Essays in Criticism*, 2, 1952, pp. 169–79; and John Paterson, '*The Mayor of Casterbridge* as Tragedy', *Victorian Studies*, 3, 1959, pp. 440–56.

11 *The Mayor of Casterbridge*, p. 354. All further references to this novel will follow the relevant quotations in the text.

12 'In Tenebris II', *Collected Poems*, p. 154.

13 *Agamemnon*, 1.250, *Greek Tragedies*, 2 vols., Volume I, edited by David Grene and Richmond Latimore, Chicago, 1960, p. 12.

14 *Tess of the D'Urbervilles*, p. 160. All further references to this novel will follow the relevant quotations in the text.

15 Cf. George Eliot's description of the effect Arthur Donnithorne's attentions have on Hetty: they produce 'a pleasant narcotic effect, making her. . .go about her work in a sort of dream'. (*Adam Bede*, I, p. 146.)

16 Cf. Sue Bridehead's comments on the shotgun wedding: 'And the other poor soul – to escape a nominal shame. . .degrading herself to the real shame of bondage to a tyrant who scorned her – a man whom to *avoid forever was her only chance of salvation.* (*Jude the Obscure*, p. 343, my italics.)

17 *Early Life*, p. 150.

18 *Ibid.*, p. 231.

19 *Early Life*, p. 224.

20 *Thomas Hardy: The Novels and Stories*, 1949, p. 152.

21 Reinhold Niebuhr, *Beyond Tragedy*, 1938, p. 164.

22 *Modern Tragedy*, 1966, p. 157 and p. 162.

23 Cf. G.B. Shaw, *Saint Joan*: 'O God, that madest this beautiful earth, when will it be ready to receive Thy saints? How long, O Lord, how long?' (Epilogue).

Chapter 6.   Henry James: Freedom and form – the tragic conflict and the novelist's dilemma

1 *The Woodlanders*, p. 15.

2 *Roderick Hudson*, p. 78 and p. 239.

3 'The Beast in the Jungle', *The Altar of the Dead, The Beast in the Jungle, The Birthplace, and Other Tales*, 1922, p. 112.

4 *Roderick Hudson*, p. 7 and p. 462.

5 'The Middle Years', *The Author of Beltraffio, The Middle Years, Greville Fane, and Other Tales*, 1922, p. 81.

6 'George Eliot's *Middlemarch*', *Galaxy*, 15, 1873, 424.

7 *The Notebooks of Henry James*, pp. 348–9.

8 'The Art of Fiction', *Longman's Magazine*, 4, 1884, 515.

9 Preface to *What Maisie Knew*, 1922, p. viii.

10 *Selected Letters*, 1877, p. 99.

11 *The American*, pp. 319–20. All further references to this novel will follow the relevant quotations in the text.

12 Preface to *The Author of Beltraffio, The Middle Years, Greville Fane, and Other Tales*, p. xiii.

13 *The Portrait of a Lady*, II, 263. All further references to this novel will follow the revevant quotations in the text.

14 Quoted by Leon Edel, *Henry James: The Untried Years 1843–1870*, 1953, p. 198.

15 *The Comic Sense of Henry James: A Study of the Early Novels*, 1960, p. 241.
16 *The Notebooks of Henry James*, 1947, p. 18.
17 *Notes of a Son and Brother*, 1914, p. 479.
18 Preface to *The Wings of the Dove*, p. vi. All further references to this novel will follow the relevant quotations in the text.
19 *Letters of Henry James*, ed. by Percy Lubbock, II, 94.

Conclusion

1 *Continuities*, 1968, p. 137.
2 *The Free Spirit: A Study of Liberal Humanism in the Novels of George Eliot, Henry James, E.M. Forster, etc.*, 1963.
3 *The Letters of John Keats*, edited by Maurice Buxton Forman, Oxford, 1935, p. 71.
4 *The Tragic Vision*, 1966, p. 4.
5 Martin Esslin, *The Theatre of the Absurd*, 1962, p. 17.
6 *Ibid.*, p. 300.

SELECT BIBLIOGRAPHY

The place of publication for all books and periodicals is London, except where otherwise stated.

I PRIMARY WORKS

(i) *Victorian literary criticism*

For the authorship of many unsigned reviews I am indebted to *The Wellesley Index to Victorian Periodicals 1824–1900*, ed. by W.E. Houghton, 2 vols., 1966–72

Anonymous review, 'The Achievements of Henry James', *Edinburgh Review*, 197 (1903), pp. 59–85
'*Daniel Deronda*', *Edinburgh Review*, 144 (1876), pp. 442–70
'*Felix Holt*', *Westminster Review*, 86 (1866), pp. 200–7
'George Eliot', *British Quarterly Review*, 45 (1867), pp. 141–78
'*The Mill on the Floss*', *The Guardian*, 25 April 1860, pp. 377–8
'*The Mill on the Floss*', *Spectator*, 7 April 1860, pp. 330–1
'Mr Henry James', *Murray's Magazine*, 10 (1891), pp. 641–54
'The Novelist's Art and Mr Henry James', *Saturday Review*, 17 January 1903, pp. 79–80
'*The Portrait of a Lady*', *Saturday Review*, 3 December 1881, pp. 703–4
'Recent Works of Fiction', *Prospective Review*, 9 April 1853, pp. 222–47
'Silver-Point Realism', *Academy*, 56 (1899), pp. 532–3

'*Tess of the D'Urbervilles*', *Bookman* (London), 1 (1892), pp. 179-80
'*The Trials of Margaret Lyndsay*', *Blackwood's Edinburgh Magazine*, 13 (1823), pp. 548-57
'Works by Mrs Oliphant', *British Quarterly Review*, 49 (1869), pp. 301-29
Arnold, Matthew, 'Preface to 1st Edition of Poems (1853)', *Irish Essays and Others*, 1904
Bagehot, Walter, *Collected Works*, ed. by Norman St John-Stevas, 8 vols., 1965, Volumes I and II, *Literary Essays*
Besant, Walter, *The Art of Fiction*, 1884
Blathwayt, Raymond, 'A Chat with the Author of *Tess*, *Black and White*, 27 August 1892, pp. 238-40
Brimley, George, *Essays*, ed. by William George Clark, 1860
Brownwell, W.C., 'Henry James', *Atlantic Monthly*, 95 (1905), p. 496-519
Bulwer-Lytton, Edward G., 'Caxtoniana', *Blackwood's Edinburgh Magazine*, 93 (1863), pp. 545-60
Courtney, W.L., *The Idea of Tragedy*, 1900
Dallas, Eneas Sweetland, *The Gay Science*, 2 vols., 1866
'*The Mill on the Floss*', *The Times*, 19 May 1860, pp. 10-11
Dowden, Edward, 'George Eliot', *Contemporary Review*, 20 (1872), pp. 403-22
'*Middlemarch* and *Daniel Deronda*', *Contemporary Review*, 29 (1877), pp. 348-69
Studies in Literature 1789-1877, 1878
Elton, Oliver, 'The Novels of Mr Henry James', *Quarterly Review*, 198 (1903), pp. 358-79
Gosse, Edmund, 'Mr Hardy's New Novel', *Cosmopolis*, 1 (1896), pp. 60-9
Harrison, Frederic, *George Eliot's Place in Literature*, 1895
Henley, W.E., '*The Europeans*', *Academy*, 14 (1868), p. 354
'New Novels', *Academy*, 22 (1882), pp. 377-8
Views and Reviews: Essays in Appreciation, 2 vols., 1890, Volume 1, *Literature*
Henneman, John Bell, 'The Dramatic Novel: George Meredith and Thomas Hardy', *Reader's Study*, 8 November 1906, pp. 680-5
Howells, W.D., *Heroines of Fiction*, 2 vols., New York, 1901
'*Jude the Obscure*', *Harper's Weekly*, 7 December 1895, p. 1156
Hutton, Richard Holt, *Brief Literary Criticisms, Selected from the 'Spectator'*, ed. by Elizabeth M. Roscoe, 1906
'*The Bostonians*', *Spectator*, 20 March 1886, pp. 388-9
'*Daniel Deronda*', *Spectator*, 9 September 1876, pp. 1131-3
'*Can You Forgive Her?*', *Spectator*, 2 September 1865, pp. 978-9
Essays on Some of the Modern Guides of English Thought in Matters of Faith, 1887

Essays Theological and Literary, 2 vols., 1871, Volume II, *Literary Essays*

'George Eliot', *Contemporary Review*, 47 (1885), pp. 372–91.

'*Middlemarch*', *Spectator*, 16 December 1871, pp. 1528–9; 3 February 1872, pp. 147–8; 30 March 1872, p. 404; 1 June 1872, pp. 685–7; 5 October 1872, pp. 1262–4 and 7 December 1872, pp. 1554–6

'*Middlemarch: A Study of Provincial Life*', *British Quarterly Review*, 57 (1873), pp. 407–29

'*Orley Farm*', *Spectator*, 11 October 1862, pp. 1136–8

'*Roderick Hudson*', *Spectator*, 5 July 1879, pp. 854–5

'*The Portrait of a Lady*', *Spectator*, 5 November 1881, pp. 1504–6

'*The Return of the Native*', *Spectator*, 8 February 1879, pp. 181–2

'*Washington Square*', *Spectator*, 5 February 1881, pp. 185–6

Jennings, L.J., '*The Portrait of a Lady*', *Quarterly Review*, 155 (1883), pp. 212–17

Kinnear, A.S., 'Mr Trollope's Novels', *North British Review*, 40 (1864), pp. 369–401

Lancaster, Henry H., *Essays and Reviews*, Edinburgh, 1876

'George Eliot's Novels', *North British Review*, 45 (1866), pp. 197–228

Le Gallienne, Richard, '*Jude the Obscure*', *Idler*, 9 (1896), pp. 114–15

Lewes, George Henry, 'A Word about *Tom Jones*', *Blackwood's Edinburgh Magazine*, 87 (1860), pp. 331–41

'Realism in Art: Recent German Fiction', *Westminster Review*, 70 (1858), pp. 488–518

'Recent Novels: French and English', *Fraser's Magazine*, 36 (1847), pp. 686–95

'Recent Tragedies', *Westminster Review*, 37 (1842), pp. 321–47

'*Strafford* and the Historical Drama', *Westminster Review*, 41 (1844), pp. 119–28

'The *Antigone* and its Critics', *Foreign Quarterly Review*, 35 (1845), pp. 56–73

'The Lady Novelists', *Westminster Review*, 58 (1852), pp. 129–41

'The Novels of Jane Austen', *Blackwood's Edinburgh Magazine*, 86 (1859), pp. 99–113

'The Principles of Success in Literature', *Fortnightly Review*, 1 (1865), pp. 85–95, pp. 185–96, pp. 572–89, and 2 (1865), pp. 257–68, and pp. 689–710

'The Rise and Fall of the European Drama', *Foreign Quarterly Review*, 35 (1845), pp. 290–334

Lockhart, J.G., '*The Five Nights of Saint Albans*', *Blackwood's Edinburgh Magazine*, 26 (1829), pp. 561–66

Massingham, H.W., 'Mr Hardy's New Novel', *Daily Chronicle*, 28 December 1891, p. 3

Masson, David, *British Novelists and their Styles*, Cambridge, 1859,

Minto, William, 'The Work of Thomas Hardy', *Bookman* (London), 1 (1891), p. 99

Moore, George, 'A Tragic Novel', *Cosmopolis*, 7 (1897), pp. 38–59

Morley, John, '*Felix Holt*', *Saturday Review*, 16 June 1866, pp. 722–4

'*Romola*', *Saturday Review*, 25 July 1863, pp. 124–5

Russell, G.W.E., *George Eliot: Her Genius and Writings*, 1882

Saintsbury, George, *Corrected Impressions: Essays on Victorian Writers*, New York, 1895

Essays in English Literature 1780–1860, 1890

A History of Nineteenth-Century Literature, 1896

'Octave Feuillet', *Fortnightly Review*, 30 (1878), pp. 102–18

'*The American*', *Academy*, 12 (1877), p. 33

'*The Tragic Muse*', *Academy*, 38 (1890), p. 148

'The Two Tragedies – a note', *Blackwood's Edinburgh Magazine*, 162 (1897), pp. 395–401

Scudder, H.E., '*The Bostonians*', *Atlantic Monthly*, 57 (1886), pp. 851–3;

'*The Portrait of a Lady*', *Atlantic Monthly*, 49 (1882), pp. 126–30

'*The Tragic Muse*', *Atlantic Monthly*, 66 (1890), pp. 419–22

Sellar, W.Y., 'Religious Novels', *North British Review*, 26 (1856), pp. 209–27

Senior, Nassau, *Essays in Fiction*, 1864

Simcox, Edith, '*Middlemarch*', *Academy*, 4 (1873), pp. 1–4

Simpson, Richard, 'George Eliot's Novels', *Home and Foreign Review*, 3 (1863), pp. 522–49

Skelton, John, 'Charlotte Brontë', *Fraser's Magazine*, 55 (1857), pp. 569–82

Smith, George Barnett, 'Our First Great Novelist', *Macmillan's Magazine*, 30 (1874), pp. 1–18

Stack, J. Herbert, 'Mr Anthony Trollope's Novels', *Fortnightly Review*, 5, New Series (1869), pp. 188–98

Stephen, Leslie, 'George Eliot', *Cornhill Magazine*, 43 (1881), pp. 152–68

Traill, Henry D., *The New Fiction*, 1897

Trollope, Anthony, 'Novel-Reading', *Nineteenth Century*, 5 (1879), pp. 24–43

Waterlow, Sydney, 'The Work of Mr Henry James', *Independent Review*, 4 (1904), pp. 236–43

Watson, William, '*Tess of the D'Urbervilles*', *Academy*, 41 (1892), pp. 125–6

Wright, Edward, 'The Novels of Thomas Hardy', *Quarterly Review*. 199 (1904), pp. 499–523

(ii) *George Eliot*

For a complete list of George Eliot's contributions to periodicals see *Essays of George Eliot*, ed. by Thomas Pinney, 1963.

'Address to Working Men, by Felix Holt', *Blackwood's Edinburgh Magazine*, 103 (1868), pp. 1–11
'The *Antigone* and its Moral', *Leader*, 29 March 1856, p. 306
'Evangelical Teaching: Dr Cumming', *Westminster Review*, 64 (1855), pp. 436–62
'The Future of German Philosophy', *Leader*, 28 July 1855, pp. 723–4
The George Eliot Letters, ed. by Gordon S. Haight, 7 vols., 1954–5
George Eliot's Life as Related in her Letters and Journals, ed. by J.W. Cross, 3 vols., 1885
'The Morality of Wilhelm Meister', *Leader*, 21 July 1855, p. 703
'The Natural History of German Life', *Westminster Review*, 66 (1856), pp. 51–79
Review of R.W. Mackay's *The Progress of the Intellect*, *Westminster Review*, 54 (1851), pp. 353–68
The Works of George Eliot, Cabinet Edition, 20 vols., Edinburgh and London, 1878–80
'Woman in France: Madame de Sablé', *Westminster Review*, 62 (1854), pp. 448–73
'Worldliness and Other-Worldliness: The Poet Young', *Westminster Review*, 67 (1857), pp. 1–42

(iii) *Thomas Hardy*

For a complete bibliography of Hardy's work see Richard Little Purdy, *Thomas Hardy: A Bibliographical Study*, 1954

Hardy, Florence E., *The Early Life of Thomas Hardy 1840–1891*, 1928
    The Later Years of Thomas Hardy 1892–1928, 1930
(Although attributed to Florence Hardy, these two volumes were largely dictated by Hardy himself.)

'Candour in English Fiction', *New Review*, 2 (1890), pp. 15–21
'The Dorsetshire Labourer', *Longman's Magazine*, 2 (1883), pp. 252–69
Letters of Thomas Hardy, ed. by Carl J. Weber, Maine, 1954
'The Profitable Reading of Fiction', *Forum*, (New York), 5 (1888), pp. 57–70
Thomas Hardy's Notebooks, ed. by Evelyn Hardy, 1955
'Why I Don't Write Plays', *Pall Mall Gazette*, 31 August 1892, p. 1
The Works of Thomas Hardy in Prose and Verse, The Wessex Edition, 24 vols., 1912–31

(iv)   *Henry James*

For a complete bibliography of James's work see Leon Edel and Dan H. Lawrence, *A Bibliography of Henry James*, 1957

'Alphonse Daudet', *Century Illustrated Monthly Magazine*, 26 (1883), pp. 498–509
'The Art of Fiction', *Longman's Magazine*, 4 (1884), pp. 502–21
'*Daniel Deronda*: A Conversation', *Atlantic Monthly*, 38 (1876), pp. 684–694
'*Far from the Madding Crowd*', *Nation*, 24 December 1874, pp. 423–4
'*Felix Holt, the Radical*', *Nation*, 16 August 1866, pp. 127–8
'George Eliot's Life', *Atlantic Monthly*, 55 (1885), pp. 668–78
'George Eliot's *Middlemarch*', *Galaxy*, 15 (1873), pp. 424–8
Henry James and H.G. Wells: A Record of their Friendship, their Debate on the Art of Fiction and their Quarrel, ed. by Leon Edel and Gordon N. Ray, 1958
Henry James and Robert Louis Stevenson: A Record of Friendship and Criticism, ed. by Janet Adam Smith, 1948
The Letters of Henry James, ed. by Percy Lubbock, 2 vols., 1920
'The Noble School of Fiction', *Nation*, 6 July 1865, pp. 21–3
The Notebooks of Henry James, ed. by F.O. Matthiesson and Kenneth B. Murdock, New York, 1947
Notes of a Son and Brother, New York, 1914
'The Novels of George Eliot', *Atlantic Monthly*, 18 (1866), pp. 479–92
The Novels and Stories of Henry James, Macmillan edition, 35 vols., 1921–3. The text is that of the New York edition, 1907–17
Selected Letters of Henry James, ed. by Leon Edel, 1956
'*The Spanish Gypsy*', *Nation*, 2 July 1868, pp. 12–14

II   SECONDARY WORKS

(i)   *George Eliot*

For a bibliography of the first 100 years of George Eliot criticism see James D. Barry, 'The Literary Reputation of George Eliot's Fiction', *Bulletin of Bibliography*, 22 (1959), pp. 176–182. Henry Auster, *Local Habitations: Regionalism in the Early Novels of George Eliot*, Cambridge, Mass., 1970, contains a useful bibliography which includes more recent criticism.

Adam, Ian, 'Character and Destiny in George Eliot's Fiction', *Nineteenth Century Fiction*, 20 (1965), pp. 127–43
Beaty, Jerome, '*Middlemarch*' from *Notebook to Novel: A Study of George Eliot's Creative Method*, Urbana, Illinois, 1960

Carroll, David, ed., *George Eliot: The Critical Heritage*, 1971
Haight, Gordon S., *George Eliot: A Biography*, 1968
   ed., *A Century of George Eliot Criticism*, 1966
Hardy, Barbara, *The Novels of George Eliot: A Study in Form*, 1959
   'Middlemarch': Critical Approaches to the Novel, 1967
Harvey, W.J., *The Art of George Eliot*, 1961
Holmstrom, John and Laurence Lerner, *George Eliot and her Readers: A Selection of Contemporary Reviews*, 1966
Knoepflmacher, U.C., *George Eliot's Early Novels: The Limits of Realism*, Berkeley, 1968
Levine, George, 'Determinism and Responsibility in the Works of George Eliot', *PMLA*, 77 (1962), pp. 268–79
Mansell, Darrell, 'George Eliot's Conception of Form', *Studies in English Literature 1500–1900*, 5 (1965), pp. 651–2
   'George Eliot's Conception of Tragedy', *Nineteenth Century Fiction*, 22 (1967), pp. 155–72
Paris, Bernard J., *Experiments in Life: George Eliot's Quest for Values*, Detroit, 1965
Rendall, Vernon, 'George Eliot and the Classics', *Notes and Queries*, 192 (1947), pp. 544–6 and 564–5
Stang, Richard, ed., *Discussions of George Eliot*, Boston, 1960
Thomson, F.C., *'Felix Holt* as Classic Tragedy', *Nineteenth Century Fiction*, 16 (1961), pp. 47–58
Yuill, W.E., 'Character is Fate', *Modern Language Review*, 57 (1962), pp. 401–2

(ii) Thomas Hardy

For a bibliography of Hardy criticism up to 1969, see *Thomas Hardy: An Annotated Bibliography of Writings about Him*, ed. by Helmut E. Gerber and W. Eugene Davis, Illinois, 1973

Abercrombie, Lascelles, *Thomas Hardy: A Critical Study*, 1912
Benvenuto, R., *'The Return of the Native* as a Tragedy in Six Books', *Nineteenth Century Fiction*, 26 (1971), pp. 83–94
Brown, Douglas, *Thomas Hardy: 'The Mayor of Casterbridge'*, 1962
Cox, R.G., ed., *Thomas Hardy: The Critical Heritage*, 1970
Dike, D.A., 'A Modern Oedipus: *The Mayor of Casterbridge*', *Essays in Criticism*, 2 (1952), pp. 169–79
Friedman, Alan, 'Thomas Hardy: Weddings be Funerals', *The Turn of the Novel*, New York, 1966, pp. 38–74
Guerard, Albert J., *Thomas Hardy: The Novels and Stories*, 1949

Hornback, Bert Gerald, *The Metaphor of Chance: Vision and Technique in the Works of Thomas Hardy*, Athens, Ohio, 1971

Johnson, Lionel, *The Art of Thomas Hardy*, 1894

Karl, F.R., '*The Mayor of Casterbridge*: A New Fiction Defined', in *Modern British Fiction*, ed. by Mark Schorer, New York, 1961

Lawrence, D.H., 'Study of Thomas Hardy', *Phoenix: The Posthumous Papers of D.H. Lawrence*, ed. by Edward Macdonald, 1936, pp. 398–516

Lerner, Laurence and John Holmstrom, *Thomas Hardy and his Readers A Selection of Contemporary Reviews*, 1968

Miller, J. Hillis, *Thomas Hardy: Distance and Desire*, 1970

Millgate, Michael, *Thomas Hardy: His Career as a Novelist*, 1971

Mizener, Arthur, '*Jude the Obscure* as a Tragedy', *Southern Review*, 6 (1940), pp. 192–213

Morrell, Roy, *Thomas Hardy: The Will and the Way*, Kuala Lumpur, 1965

Paterson, John, *The Making of 'The Return of the Native'*, California, 1960

    'Hardy, Faulkner and the Prosaics of Tragedy', *Centennial Review*, 5 (1961), pp. 156–75

    '*The Mayor of Casterbridge* as Tragedy', *Victorian Studies*, 3 (1959), pp. 440–56

Rutland, W.R., *Thomas Hardy: A Study of his Writings and their Background*, Oxford, 1938

Tanner, Tony, 'Colour and Movement in Hardy's *Tess of the D'Urbervilles*', *Critical Quarterly*, 10 (1968), pp. 219–39

Wing, George, 'Tess and the Romantic Milkmaid', *Review of English Literature*, 3 (1962), pp. 22–30

(iii)   *Henry James*

For a bibliography of James criticism see *Henry James: A Bibliography of Secondary Works*, edited by Beatrice Ricks, New Jersey, 1975

Andreas, Osborn, *Henry James and the Expanding Horizon: A Study of the Meaning and Basic Themes of James's Fiction*, Seattle, 1948

Barzun, Jacques, 'James the Melodramatist', *Kenyon Review*, 5 (1943), pp. 508–21

Blackmur, R.P., 'The Loose and Baggy Monsters of Henry James', *The Lion and the Honeycomb: Essays in Solicitude and Critique*, 1956, pp. 268–88

Conrad, Joseph, 'Henry James: An Appreciation', *Notes on Life and Letters*, 1905, pp. 13–23

Crews, Frederick C., *The Tragedy of Manners: Moral Drama in the Later Novels of Henry James*, 1957

Fergusson, Francis, 'James's Idea of Dramatic Form', *Kenyon Review*, 5 (1943), pp. 495–507

Ford, Ford Madox, *Henry James: A Critical Study*, 1913

Galloway, David, '*The Portrait of a Lady*', 1967

Gard, Roger, ed., *Henry James: The Critical Heritage*, 1968

Goldsmith, A.L., 'Henry James's Reconciliation of Free Will and Determinism', *Nineteenth Century Fiction*, 13 (1958), pp. 109–26

Holland, Laurence Bedwell, *The Expense of Vision: Essays on the Craft of Henry James*, Princeton, 1964

Isle, Walter Whitfield, *Experiments in Form: Henry James's Novels 1896–1901*, Cambridge, Mass., 1968

Krook, Dorothea, *The Ordeal of Consciousness in Henry James*, Cambridge, 1962

Lerner, Daniel and Oscar Cargill, 'Henry James at the Grecian Urn', *PMLA*, 66 (1951), pp. 316–31

Leyburn, E.D., *Strange Alloy: The Relation of Comedy to Tragedy in the Fiction of Henry James*, Chapel Hill, 1968

Matthiesson, F.O., *Henry James: The Major Phase*, 1946

Poirier, Richard, *The Comic Sense of Henry James: A Study of the Early Novels*, 1960

Pound, Ezra, 'Brief Note', *Little Review*, 5 (1918), pp. 6–9

Segal, Ora, *The Lucid Reflector: The Observer in Henry James's Fiction*, 1969

Spender, Stephen, 'Henry James and the Contemporary Subject', *The Destructive Element: A Study of Modern Writers and Beliefs*, 1935, pp. 189–200

Ward, Joseph Anthony, *The Imagination of Disaster: Evil in the Fiction of Henry James*, Lincoln, 1961

(iv) *Background reading*

Bennett, E.K., 'The Novelle as a Substitute for Tragedy', *A History of the German Novelle*, Cambridge, 1934

Chesterton, G.K., *The Victorian Age in Literature*, 1947

Cox, C.B., *The Free Spirit: A Study of Liberal Humanism in the Novels of George Eliot, Henry James, E.M. Forster, etc.*, 1963

Esslin, Martin, *The Theatre of the Absurd*, 1962

Fergusson, Francis, *The Idea of a Theatre*, Princeton, 1949

Graham, Kenneth, *English Criticism of the Novel 1865–1900*, Oxford, 1965

Hardy, Barbara, *The Appropriate Form: An Essay on the Novel*, 1964

Holloway, John, *The Victorian Sage: Studies in Argument*, 1953

Jaspers, Karl, *Tragedy is Not Enough*, 1953

Kermode, Frank, *Continuities*, 1968

Krieger, Murray, *The Tragic Vision*, Chicago, 1966

Lerner, Laurence, *The Truthtellers: Jane Austen, George Eliot, D.H. Lawrence*, 1967

Lewis, C.S., *Experiment in Criticism*, Cambridge, 1961

Miller, Arthur, 'Tragedy and the Common Man', *New York Times*, 27 February 1949, sec. 2, pp. 1 and 3

Niebuhr, Reinhold, *Beyond Tragedy: Essays on the Christian Interpretation of History*, 1938

Praz, Mario, *The Hero in Eclipse in Victorian Fiction*, 1956

Rosenberg, Harold, 'Character Change and the Drama', *The Tradition of the New*, New York, 1959, pp. 135–153

Speirs, John, *Poetry towards Novel*, 1971

Stang, Richard, *The Theory of the Novel in England 1850–1870*, 1959

Steiner, George, *The Death of Tragedy*, 1961

Stevenson, Lionel, ed., *Victorian Fiction: A Guide to Research*, Cambridge, Mass., 1964

Van Ghent, Dorothy, *The English Novel: Form and Function*, New York, 1953

Williams, Raymond, *The English Novel from Dickens to Lawrence*, 1970
Modern Tragedy, 1966
'Realism and the Contemporary Novel', *The Long Revolution*, 1961, pp. 274–89

INDEX

The word 'quoted' before a page reference indicates that the title of the work does not appear on that page, but at the end of the book in the note mentioned after the page number.